A Community of Equals

NEW DEMOCRACY FORUM

A
Community
of Equals

THE CONSTITUTIONAL
PROTECTION OF NEW AMERICANS

Owen Fiss

Foreword by EDWIDGE DANTICAT

Edited by Joshua Cohen and Joel Rogers
for *Boston Review*

BEACON PRESS

BOSTON

BEACON PRESS
25 Beacon Street
Boston, Massachusetts 02108-2892
www.beacon.org

Beacon Press books are published under the auspices of the
Unitarian Universalist Association of Congregations.

05 04 03 02 01 00 99   8 7 6 5 4 3 2 1

This book is printed on recycled acid-free paper that contains at least 20
percent postconsumer waste and meets the uncoated paper ANSI/NISO
specifications for permanence as revised in 1992.

Text design by Christopher Kuntze
Composition by Wilsted & Taylor Publishing Services

Library of Congress Cataloging-in-Publication Data

Fiss, Owen M.
    A community of equals : the constitutional protection of new
Americans / Owen Fiss.
        p.   cm. — (New democracy forum)
    Includes bibliographical references.
    ISBN 0-8070-0437-5 (pa)
    1. Emigration and immigration law—United States.   2. Civil
rights—United States.   3. Aliens—United States.   I. Series.
KF4819.F57   1999
342.73'082—DC21   98-52826

For

Thurgood Marshall

an inspiration for all the world

Contents

Foreword

*I*n recent years, immigration has become one of the most heavily debated issues in the United States. The acute desire to close American borders to new arrivals, mostly persons of color from developing countries, has . surfaced in school board gatherings, town hall meetings, gubernatorial races, even presidential elections. In 1994, the passing of California's Proposition 187 threatened to make spies of the Immigration and Naturalization Service out of all public school teachers, hospital employees, and social service providers, encouraging them to surrender to the INS all undocumented aliens who came to them requesting educational, medical, or financial assistance. Unfortunately, these days, "The Immigrant as Pariah"—the title of Owen Fiss's essay—is not only a stinging theoretical premise, but also a very harsh reality.

I am an immigrant myself and the child of immigrants. In the 1970s, my family left Haiti and came to the United States looking for a better life. Like most newcomers, we had no idea what would await us here, but hoped that it would be better than the repression of the dictatorship and the arduous poverty we had left behind.

We were far from unique in our confidence in the ideals of the American dream, our belief that Lady Liberty's call, "Give me your tired, your poor, . . ." was a sincere and honest invitation and welcome.

I thought of my own family as I read Fiss's essay and the responses to it, particularly the arguments concerning "(a) bars on employment; (b) exclusions from public schools; and (c) denials of statutory entitlements . . ." Though my parents, because of their own sense of non-entitlement and embarrassment, would have been averse to using the financial handouts of the state, they certainly would have been forced to had they not been able to work. And if I had not been able to attend school, I certainly would never have gotten the education that now allows me to write these very simple words.

The essays here raise several meaningful questions, including many that will certainly incite even more inquiry and debate. Does America still see itself as the "land of immigrants"? Why not, if only "to preserve our society as a community of equals,"[1] invest in the survival and progress of all immigrants? Making them pariahs will not force immigrants to pick up and leave. They will continue to work hard in spite of the obstacles, which, though major, probably constitute better conditions than the ones they left behind. What we must fear most is the effect that the more severe disabilities would have on the children of immigrants, the ones who feel that they belong to this country that threatens to keep them out of its schools and to not treat them when they are ill. We must have a better hope for these children than that they would further swell the ranks of America's poor and later collect—with interest—on the services that some would not have us provide for them now.

It used to be that an immigrant was one who assimilated quickly and disappeared joyfully into America's melting pot. These days immigrants are transnational, global ambassadors for both the country they live in and the one they've moved from. Even as they pay taxes and contribute to the economic structure in the United States, they also build schools and clinics and support businesses in the countries of their birth, helping to rebuild the fabric that forced their own migration and possibly slowing down the exodus of others.

Is the United States completely color-blind when it comes to immigration? Is our immigration policy purged of ethnic and racist bias when Haitian immigrants lingered in detention centers and tent cities on military bases while Cubans and Eastern Europeans were allowed free entry to the United States? I too would like to think that at the heart of America's immigration policy is an acknowledgment of its own history as a country built and rebuilt by the labor of—among others—poor workers from abroad. One would think that the great contributions of past immigrants would temper the venomous arguments that reduce some of the most vulnerable and most often exploited members of our society to pariahs and pests. However, this is not yet the case. From this perspective, it isn't too much to ask that new immigrants receive the same very "basic decency that each of us owes to others within the community."[2] As we have learned from the past, it can only be returned a hundredfold.

Editors' Preface

JOSHUA COHEN AND JOEL ROGERS

*D*emocracy, Lincoln said, is government of, by, and for the people. What happens when immigrants come to a country but have not yet attained the status of citizens—when they are not yet part of the people? Should democracy also be for them?

In the United States, these old questions of democratic thought are made newly urgent by the large numbers of recent immigrants and by state and federal measures discriminating against them. Changes in federal welfare law since 1996, for example, exclude both legal and illegal immigrants from welfare benefits. Proponents of such exclusions argue that they are a reasonable way to discourage immigration by the impoverished and reduce fiscal burdens on the states. They claim that we have limited obligations to non-members—no greater than our obligations to people outside the territory. Critics argue that exclusions represent simple exploitation of a vulnerable group whose members lack sufficient economic or political power to protect themselves.

Owen Fiss belongs to the company of critics. A distinguished professor of constitutional law, Fiss has long argued that our Constitution—in particular the Equal Protection Clause—is most fundamentally a design of democratic community. Whereas commentators all agree that the constitutional guarantee of "equal protection of the laws" condemns discrimination, Fiss goes further, urging that it also bans group subordination, as incompatible with democratic community.

In "The Immigrant as Pariah," Fiss applies this anti-subordination principle to the treatment of immigrants under current federal welfare law. According to Fiss, by providing equal protection for all persons residing within our borders (not just citizens), the Constitution commands that there shall be no subordinate caste, however constructed or populated, within these United States. Thus, while our Constitution may be silent on how much we should open our borders or whether non-citizens should have voting rights, it requires equality in the provision of basic social benefits for citizens and non-citizens alike. Failure to provide social benefits to non-citizens dishonors "our society as a community of equals."

Framed as an essay in constitutional theory and political morality, "The Immigrant as Pariah" is also a critique of the current state of American politics. Fiss thinks political discourse and political organization in the country are now so feeble, so corrupt, that only the Supreme Court—an institution insulated from popular opinion—can rescue the Republic, can save it from degenerating into a society of citizen insiders dominating an oppressed class of immigrant pariahs. So a forum that begins as a debate about immigration turns into a broader argument about the state of American democracy: Is it now so distorted in its electoral workings that "the people" will fulfill our constitutional obligations to non-members only if we get dragged into court?

I

The Immigrant as Pariah

OWEN FISS

*I*mmigration is an issue of concern to all the nations of the world, but it has a special meaning for the United States because we are a nation of immigrants. In the eighteenth century, most of the continent belonged to Indian tribes and Mexicans living in the western states, but of the 270 million persons that now constitute the United States, only a very small number can trace their roots to these groups. The country is now largely populated by persons whose ancestors immigrated to it. Some came in chains (the African slaves), but most came out of choice, to avoid famines and wars or simply in search of economic and social betterment.

To this very day, the doors of the United States have remained open. Last year almost one million immigrants were admitted for permanent residence. This number is vastly smaller than the number of those wanting to immigrate, and arguably fewer people than the country might support economically or socially, but I take a measure of pride in the fact that we admit as many as we do and that since the 1960s our immigration laws have been purged of an overt racial and ethnic bias. The

{ 3 }

national origins quota has been abolished, and today we have specific programs designed to promote diversity among those admitted. These features of the law pay tribute to our history as a nation of immigrants. What is new, and at odds with this history, is that we have increasingly imposed disabilities on immigrants, mostly on illegal immigrants, but even on those who are lawfully present.

POLITICAL VERSUS SOCIAL DISABILITIES

One form of disability—let's call it political—is deeply rooted in our culture and strikes me as acceptable. Here I am thinking principally of laws restricting to citizens the right to vote. At its core, becoming a naturalized citizen involves affirming one's loyalty to the Constitution, and such an affirmation seems an unobjectionable requirement for participating in those activities such as voting that are responsible for sustaining or implementing the political principles that define the nation.

At one point in our history, some states allowed aliens to vote. It is also true that many immigrants who reside in the country for a long time may come to feel a similar loyalty to the Constitution and the political principles under which they happen to live. Yet as long as naturalization remains a viable and fairly economical option, as it indeed is in the United States—last year more than one million immigrants became citizens—it seems sensible for the law to require completion of the formal process of affirmation before granting immigrants the right to vote.

The more troublesome form of disability is social as opposed to political. In recent years the social disabilities imposed upon immigrants have increased, and have taken three different forms: (a) bars on employment, (b) exclusions from public schools, and (c) denials of statutory entitlements, such as food stamps or medical services, that are routinely provided to the poor by the welfare state.

Many of these disabilities were imposed by individual states and could be seen as a fiscal adjustment to federalism. In America, both the formulation and implementation of immigration policy are in the hands of the federal government. Social services are generally provided by the states, and a number of states, principally California and Texas, imposed social disabilities on illegal aliens as a way of protecting themselves financially from the failure of the federal government adequately to police the nation's borders. The number of illegal immigrants is estimated to be about five million, and almost three million of these reside in the states bordering Mexico.

In March 1998, a federal district judge in Los Angeles struck down a California law—the notorious Proposition 187, adopted by popular referendum in 1994—that denied almost all state services, including medical care, to illegal immigrants. The Los Angeles court found that this law intrudes upon the exclusive jurisdiction over immigration reserved to the federal government by the Constitution. This ruling may not survive an appeal, which remains pending, and in any event provides no protection against analogous federal enactments, some of which followed closely on the heels of Proposition 187.

Federal statutes had already barred illegal immigrants from working, but in 1996 Congress enacted a provision analogous to Proposition 187 but far more severe. As part of its welfare reform agenda, Congress denied certain welfare benefits, including food stamps and financial support for the aged and disabled, to all immigrants, legal or illegal. Indeed, this legislation—the Personal Responsibility and Work Opportunity Reconciliation Act of 1996—even cut off the benefits of those immigrants lawfully admitted to the United States before the date of its enactment, August 22, 1996.

This unusual retroactive feature proved to be too much for Congress, and it soon had second thoughts. In August 1997, Congress enacted a measure to restore certain benefits to the infirm and aged who had been admitted to the United States before August 22, 1996, and in June 1998 it passed a measure providing food stamps for select categories of immigrants—children, the elderly, and the disabled—who had been lawfully admitted to the United States before that same date.

These amendments took some of the edge off the 1996 welfare act, but the basic regime introduced by that law

—no welfare benefits for immigrants, even those law-fully admitted—remains intact and has brought to the fore many issues of law and policy relating to immigration. For me, it raised with special urgency and clarity the question of whether enactments imposing social disabilities on immigrants can be squared with the Constitution, particularly the provision that guarantees to all persons—not all citizens, but all persons—equal protection of the laws.

THE CONSTITUTIONAL RULE

In addressing this question, lawyers and commentators have turned to the now familiar rule that bars arbitrary discrimination. This rule has emerged over the last century as a gloss on equal protection and has in fact been used as a powerful aid for the protection of minorities and women. The temptation is therefore great to use this rule to protect immigrants, yet such an effort seems misplaced.

The laws imposing social disabilities on immigrants do indeed seem at odds with the Constitution, but only because of the social stratification they tend to produce, not because they violate the antidiscrimination principle. The constitutional guarantee of equality bars not just discrimination, but also laws that create or perpetuate caste-like social structures, and for that reason calls into question the 1996 welfare act and similar measures.

Antidiscrimination is essentially individualistic. It guarantees individual fairness in the award of a scarce opportunity, say a job, and demands that individual applicants be selected on the basis of criteria that are functionally related to some legitimate purpose of the relevant institution. The principle is given practical effect in the law through the construction of a short list of criteria—the so-called suspect criteria—that presumptively are not related to any such purpose. Race is the paradigm of a suspect criterion because we assume that an individual's race or color is never, or almost never, functionally related to the pursuit of any legitimate purpose. This assumption about the irrelevance of race undergirds and gives continuing vitality to Justice Harlan's now famous aphorism "Our Constitution is color-blind."

In recent years, many have come to question the general presumption about the irrelevance of race. We have discovered that a certain measure of color consciousness, as exemplified by affirmative action and school desegregation remedies, is necessary to eradicate the legacy of slavery and Jim Crow. As a result, we have grown uneasy with antidiscrimination as the sole strategy for dealing with race. In the case of immigrants, however, the inadequacy of antidiscrimination seems even more glaring because we cannot engage any general presumption about the irrelevance of alienage, which is commonly employed in a wide variety of legal processes, many of which seem of unquestionable validity. Indeed, drawing a distinction between aliens and citizens is integral to the effort of any sovereign nation to determine its own membership. It is essential to the very existence of the nation as a community.

Although no blanket judgment can be entertained as to the irrelevance of alienage, there may be particular cases where it is in fact irrelevant. In these cases, a court might conclude that distinguishing between aliens and citizens serves no legitimate end, but rather is an expression of a hatred or dislike of immigrants, or, in the words of contemporary legal doctrine, an expression of an "animus." This highly contextualized version of the antidiscrimination principle might be similar to the rule now applied to handicapped persons, but would be qualitatively different from that which over the years has protected blacks or even women. For them, antidiscrimination has had a near universalistic reach. Even more, in contrast to the rule used to protect blacks or women, the particularized version of antidiscrimination now proposed for immigrants would be devoid of any real bite. It would rarely invalidate a law.

There is no denying that, as a purely psychological matter, anti-immigrant sentiment is pervasive in America, but that is not the issue. A statute should never be judged on the basis of actual motivation, for then the validity of the law would depend on an inquiry into the minds of the legislators—never an easy or welcomed endeavor for a coordinate branch of government. Such an inquiry would also require some method for aggregating the good and bad motivations of the multitude of legislators, and it might yield anomalous results. A statute might be struck down if it were adjudged to be the product of a political process in which animus entered, but the same statute might be allowed to stand if the legislators were perceived to have a different, more benign, motivation. For these reasons, laws should be judged on the basis of social purpose objectively conceived, not actual motivation, and from that perspective it would be hard to challenge a law imposing disabilities on immigrants as constituting an arbitrary discrimination. A legitimate social purpose can almost always be imagined.

A COURT DECISION

To demonstrate why antidiscrimination is inadequate in this context, and to lay the foundation for the shift to a more structural approach, let me take up a case decided by the Supreme Court in 1982, *Plyler v. Doe*. This case involved a Texas regulation denying children who were illegal immigrants free admission to elementary and secondary schools. All children born in the United States, even those of parents who are illegally present, are by virtue of the Fourteenth Amendment citizens of this country. Yet if children who were born abroad immigrate to the United States illegally, either alone or, more plausibly, with their parents, they would themselves be regarded as illegal aliens. It was children such as these that the Texas law sought to exclude from local schools.

No one would deny that as a purely historical matter there was a lot of anti-immigrant animus in Texas when the state legislature enacted the law challenged in *Plyler*. It also seems fair to say that this hatred or fear played a role in the causal dynamic that produced the regulation. Yet the Texas law could not be invalidated under the antidiscrimination principle because it could be rationally justified as means to serve a legitimate social purpose, specifically, to discourage the influx of illegal immigrants into the state. Arguably, there may have been other ways of achieving this end—increasing the barriers on the border or increasing the sanctions of the criminal law for illegal entry, for example—though none of these measures were available to the state of Texas as opposed to the federal government. But the antidiscrimination principle itself does not require the state to select the best means available for pursuit of a legitimate end. Antidiscrimination promises individual fairness, not state efficiency, and is satisfied if the criterion for distinguishing among individuals is functionally related, even weakly, to a legitimate end.

To regulate the choice of means by the state of Texas another theory was needed, and in its ruling on the *Plyler* case, the Court found it in the rule prohibiting any state from creating, in Justice Brennan's terms, a "subclass of illiterates." On this reading, the Equal Protection Clause prohibits not only discrimination, but also the creation of a near-caste structure. It prohibits creating socially and economically disadvantaged groups that are forced to live at the margin of society, isolated from the mainstream, always at risk, seen in their own eyes and in those of the dominant group as inferior.

Over the last fifteen years, *Plyler* has remained good law, but there has been some debate as to the scope of the ruling and its underlying principle. Some of this controversy has been fueled by certain passages of Brennan's opinion for the Court, which are more keyed to antidiscrimination than antisubjugation. A question has also been raised as to whether the case is limited to the protection of children. Brennan spoke movingly of the children, and one of the justices whose vote was necessary for the judgment—Justice Powell—saw the school-age children as the principal victims of the Texas law and made their alleged innocence the basis for intervention. Admittedly, these children were illegally present in the United States, but they were brought here by their parents and thus, Powell reasoned, not responsible for any wrongdoing.

This concern with "innocent victims" is a constant and pervasive theme in Justice Powell's jurisprudence. It surfaced most dramatically in his effort to place limits on affirmative action programs in the name of antidiscrimination—and no wonder, since it partakes of the individualism that gives life to the antidiscrimination principle. In the family context, however, this individualism seems especially misplaced, since it is so hard to allocate responsibility within that social unit. True, parents may have made the decision to cross the border, but they may have done that to improve the life chances of their children. Thus, although the children did not choose to enter, they may have been the reason for the illegal entry and in some sense responsible for it. Choice is not the only basis for allocating responsibility, especially within the family.

I also find it difficult to understand why the constitutional validity of the Texas regulation should turn on the alleged innocence of the victims. Under the antidiscrimination principle the fault of the excluded group may be of relevance, on the (questionable) assumption that it is permissible for a government to allocate benefits only to the "morally worthy" or those not guilty of wrongdoing. Yet fault is of no relevance under the antisubjugation principle, for what that principle tests for is not the fairness of an allocative rule but the social structure that such a rule creates. No one, innocent or not, should be transformed by the state into a pariah in the way that exclusion from schools would do.

To give substance to this intuition, imagine a public education system in Texas that ran an adult literacy program for all the community, but which barred illegal aliens. The targeted group chose to enter illegally, and thus are responsible for their status. They are not, in Powell's terms, "innocent." Yet I would insist that the same result of *Plyler* should follow in such a case. Excluding illegal aliens from this program severely disadvantages them economically and socially and creates the very same danger that moved the Court in *Plyler*—the establishment of a subclass of illiterates. The fact that the immigrants in question have violated the law in coming here is irrelevant to this conclusion.

Others who have sought to limit *Plyler* have emphasized that the case involved elementary and secondary education. They draw their inspiration from the concurrences of Justices Blackmun and Marshall, yet fail to articulate any principled basis for limiting the case in this way. In some state constitutions, elementary and secondary education is singled out for special protection. The federal constitution does not, however, have any special provision for education, and it has long been held—in a decision that Blackmun joined but from which Marshall dissented—that no such right is implied. The judgment in *Plyler* did not presuppose that there was a federal constitutional right to education. As in *Brown v. Board of Education*, the Court's emphasis was on the functional as opposed to the formal significance of public education, and on what it might mean for a group of people to be excluded from it.

A STRUCTURAL APPROACH

Once we take a functional perspective, we can well understand why the antisubjugation principle should reach beyond education and guard against exclusion from all manner of state programs, including food stamps, public housing, and medical treatment. Illiteracy is a severe disability in modern society, but perhaps no more so than being malnourished or homeless or sick and in need of medical attention. The state routinely responds to these needs of its citizens, and against this background the exclusion of immigrants has a severely subordinating effect upon them.

So too do laws that bar illegal immigrants from working. These laws typically operate by imposing criminal sanctions on employers who hire illegal aliens. Once again, the border states were the prime movers in this domain, and in 1976 the Supreme Court upheld a California law penalizing those who hire illegal aliens. The Court reasoned that such a law is within the authority of the states because it relates to matters of only local concern. By 1986, the federal government moved in and imposed its own general ban. Today, laws prohibiting the employment of illegal immigrants are a familiar part of the legal landscape and are assumed to be of unquestionable validity. Yet they should be seen as having the same subordinating effect as the law condemned in *Plyler*, which, recall, was also aimed at illegal aliens. These laws force illegal immigrants into underground sweatshops or to survive by begging or stealing and thus to live at the margins of society—no education, no welfare, no work.

In calling into question laws excluding immigrants from welfare and educational programs and barring them from working, I am not surreptitiously questioning the validity of laws regulating the admission of immigrants to this country. For present purposes, I am prepared to assume that these laws are just, and further that the availability of jobs, welfare benefits, and public education may provide incentives for illegal entry. My point is not to subvert the admission process or otherwise open the borders, but rather to insist that laws regarding admission cannot be enforced or implemented in ways that would transform immigrants into pariahs. Admission laws can be enforced by fences at the borders, deportation proceedings, or criminal sanctions, not, I maintain, by imposing social disabilities.

From a purely individualistic perspective this may seem an oddity. If put to the choice between deportation or a life in the United States without education or welfare or work the individual immigrant might well choose the latter. He or she may well prefer to live a marginal existence in the United States rather than to return to the country from which he or she came, and there may be good and sufficient reasons for that choice. A pariah in San Diego may live a lot better life than a citizen of Guatemala.

This fact—if it is a fact—may have a great deal of relevance for the theory of rational choice, but not for the proper construction of the Constitution, for the Constitution is not a set of rules to maximize individual welfare on some global scale. Rather, it is a statement about how a society wishes to organize itself, and prohibits subjugation, even voluntary subjugation, because such a practice would disfigure society. In that respect, the antisubjugation principle of the Fourteenth Amendment is analogous to the Thirteenth Amendment's ban on slavery, which precludes not only forced slavery but also selling oneself into slavery or choosing to become a slave. Both amendments seek to prevent the emergence of social practices that are at odds with the egalitarianism to which the Constitution aspires. We ought not to subjugate immigrants, not because we owe them anything, but to preserve our society as a community of equals.

The Constitution does not condemn all distinctions between people, say between the rich and the poor or between the smart and the dumb. The subjugation produced by the laws imposing social disabilities on immigrants is, however, of another character, for what is entailed is not simply drawing a distinction among people but rather creating a different kind of social structure altogether. Laws imposing social disabilities on immigrants entail a further stratification or degradation of the very poor or, in Justice Brennan's words, raise the specter of creating "a permanent caste." Not all immigrants are poor; not all illegal immigrants are poor; but the laws in question take their toll on the poor and compound the disadvantages that come from poverty. These laws further isolate poor immigrants from the dominant groups in our society and make them vulnerable in a way that laws which privilege intelligence or wealth do not. Those immigrants who ordinarily count on working, or using the public schools, or who sometimes need to fall back on welfare, stand in danger of being turned into pariahs.

In some cases, the process of degradation is facilitated by other marks, such as race. Although the *Plyler* Court did not dwell on this fact, it well knew that the illegal immigrants targeted by the Texas regulation were from Mexico and thus suffered from the degradation that all people of color suffer in the United States. But race seems to be only an aggravating factor, not essential to the harm. Even if the illegal immigrants were not from Mexico, or Asia, or Africa but were from Canada, or Ireland, or any one of a number of Northern European countries, the danger would exist that these people—not defined by race or even national origin, but by their legislative or cultural designation as immigrants—would be isolated from the dominant groups in society and treated as inferior. They would become the new underclass.

POLITICAL VULNERABILITY

A rule protecting immigrants against social disabilities may seem inconsistent with my willingness to accept political disabilities, for denying the right to vote to aliens may also isolate them and make them vulnerable to the dominant group. I acknowledge that, as a purely moral matter, the political and social disabilities might be indistinguishable, yet from the perspective of the Constitution there is a crucial difference (comparable to the one that necessitated two separate constitutional amendments to set the record straight on race—the Thirteenth, to abolish slavery, and the Fifteenth, to confer the right to vote on blacks.) The social disabilities are unconstitutional because they create a social structure that is inconsistent with the conception of community embodied in the Constitution. The political disabilities, in contrast, are not inconsistent with that conception of community; indeed, as I said at the outset, they are an expression of it. The political disabilities rest on the idea that the nation is a community, not just a geographically bounded territory, and, like any such voluntary organization, this community requires rules of membership and vests the power of governance in those lawfully admitted to membership.

For these reasons, I would draw a distinction in the constitutional realm between social and political disabilities. One can recognize the distinction between citizen and non-citizen in the political realm without turning the latter into a pariah. The legitimacy of political disabilities does not legitimate social disabilities. In fact, the very allowance of political disablement—confining the right to vote to citizens—is a good and sufficient reason, constitutionally or even as a matter of democratic theory, for the judiciary to scrutinize with a healthy measure of skepticism the work of the elected bodies insofar as it affects immigrants.

Over the last thirty or forty years, certain groups, above all blacks, have received a special measure of protection from the judiciary. Not all laws disadvantaging them have been invalidated—far from it—but the courts have not let these laws stand without undertaking an exacting inquiry into whether they can be reconciled with the relevant constitutional principle (commonly antidiscrimination). To some extent, this special attentiveness can be seen as a measure of corrective justice, as an implicit atonement for the wrongs admittedly done to African-Americans in the past. Immigrants cannot easily appeal to considerations of corrective justice. As an abstract category, immigrants have long been subject to abuse, but as actual people they are mostly newcomers.

On the other hand, they are very much entitled to claim the benefit of the more instrumental rationale for judicial solicitude—political powerlessness.

Immigrants who are not citizens are a numerical minority. Some can count on people of similar national origins who are citizens to voice their concerns, but that is exceptional. For the most part, they encounter great difficulties in forming the coalitions that are the mainstay of politics, since all the others can gain by shunning them. In that sense, aliens, like blacks, are a discrete and insular minority, yet their powerlessness has another and more dramatic dimension—they are denied the vote. They are excluded, openly and formally, from the electoral process and for that reason make a very special claim to the protection of our courts of law.

Therefore, rather than justifying social disabilities, the political disabilities immigrants suffer stand as a powerful reason why the one institution that stands above the political fray—the judiciary—should make doubly certain that the life of an immigrant, never an easy matter, is not more difficult than it has to be. The Constitution denies the majority the power to turn any group into a pariah, and the burden properly falls on the courts to make this rule, to borrow a phrase Brennan coined in still another context, a living truth.

❖ II ❖

Let the People Decide

RICHARD B. FREEMAN

Should someone who enters the United States *illegally* receive the same legal rights and social benefits as legal residents? Should someone who enters the United States *legally* as an immigrant receive less in the way of social transfers than someone who is native born? If, with Owen Fiss, one accepts the principle that a sovereign nation must distinguish between aliens and citizens, illegal and legal immigrants, these questions do not permit clear yes or no answers.

You may harbor anti-immigrant sentiments, as Fiss believes many Americans do, but still recognize that protection from crime, judicial due process, and national labor laws must include illegal immigrants. Once people are here, the legal system must protect them. There can be no "hunting license" for natives to prey on illegal immigrants. On the other hand, you may have pro-immigrant inclinations, as many Americans do, but still be hard-pressed to defend an employer who sacks citizens to hire illegal immigrants or who applies affirmative action preferences to minority immigrants.

Policy decisions are made in the gray area between these extremes. What factors can help guide us?

The first factor is the effects of the policy on the electorate's well-being. Part of this is economic. Simple economics argues that the state should be less generous to immigrants than to the existing electorate. If tax-funded benefits are strictly private goods, with no impact beyond the direct beneficiary, why should citizens give those benefits to non-citizens, much less to illegal aliens?

But many tax-funded benefits have spillovers. If immigrants live in unhealthy conditions, disease may spread; if they are poorly educated, national productivity may suffer; if they have poor employment chances, they may commit crimes. Programs that reduce these adverse outcomes may benefit even the most narrow-minded citizen.

The second factor is the effects of policy on the well-being of the immigrant, legal or illegal. We may favor giving some benefits to immigrants because we care about how they fare. We may choose to help illegal immigrants who are hardworking members of our community because they are outstanding human beings.

Fiss wants the judiciary to draw a boundary in the gray area in favor of immigrants, because the Equal Protection Clause of the Constitution prohibits "the creation of a near caste-structure ... [with] socially and economically disadvantaged groups that ... live at the margin of society," and immigrants are exceptionally likely to fall into this category. He favors restricting the ballot, but not much else, to citizens, and makes little distinction between legal and illegal immigrants. Nowhere does he consider the fact that more funds spent on immigrants may mean fewer funds spent on disadvantaged natives or that more spending on illegal immigrants may mean less spending on legal immigrants.

I find his arguments strained and reject as antidemocratic the notion that the judiciary should determine policy in this area. We may all oppose social exclusion, but to argue that the Constitution requires that courts regulate social policies to limit such exclusion seems to me to be an extraordinary reading of law. Fiss argues that immigrants should have a special place in social policy because they are "in danger of being turned into pariahs" whereas poor natives face no such problem, that because immigrants do not vote they merit special judicial protection. But surely he knows that many immigrants are highly educated with high incomes, whereas many Americans from disadvantaged groups are poorly educated with low incomes. The implication that the "social disabilities" of being an immigrant exceed those of being poor in the United States misses completely the bifurcation of the U.S. income distribution between rich and poor.

In some instances I agree with Fiss about where we

ought to draw the boundary between what we do for aliens and what we do for citizens. But in all instances I would leave the decision in the hands of the electorate.

Fiss argues that a state should not exclude illegal immigrants from taxpayer-funded adult literacy programs on the grounds that their having "violated the law in coming here is irrelevant" to their eligibility. I disagree. Citizens can legitimately decide that the benefits of increasing the literacy of illegal immigrants outweigh the costs (and I would so decide), but surely citizens can legitimately decide the opposite.

Fiss argues against imposing criminal sanctions on employers for hiring illegal aliens, because such sanctions will force the illegal aliens to live at the margins of society. But what about the citizens and legal immigrants who might otherwise have held those jobs? Under Fiss's analysis, it is legitimate to push *them* to the margins of society because they don't bear the special mark of an illegal immigrant. But if you tell employers that they are free to hire illegal workers, they or market intermediaries will provide an ever-increasing supply of such workers, and we will end up with more, not fewer, people at the bottom of the income distribution.

Fiss recognizes that the end result of his analysis is that the nation would be left with only "fences at the border, deportation proceedings, [and] criminal sanctions" to deal with illegal immigrants. Logically he cannot object to such measures and policies, and he does not. But surely it is more sensible and humane to make finer gradations to decide that some tax moneys may go to people who enter illegally while other moneys cannot be spent on them, that legal immigrants should have greater access to social programs than illegal immigrants but less access than natives. The right place to argue over the eligibility of non-citizens for various social benefits is in Congress or state legislatures.

What most disturbs me about Fiss's article is the notion that immigrants are somehow so "socially disabled," that they need special judicial intervention to keep them from becoming a low-level caste of pariahs. I see the opposite: immigrant communities that are a vibrant addition to our nation, and millions of skilled and hardworking immigrants succeeding in the mainstream economy. The key defining aspect of America is not immigrant status. It is income. Our community of equals is threatened not by immigrants nor by their eligibility for particular social programs but by our income distribution.

First Class

T. ALEXANDER ALEINIKOFF

*M*ore than two decades ago, Owen Fiss made a major contribution to constitutional theory with the unveiling of his antisubjugation approach to equal protection analysis. Fiss's focus on status harms to specially disadvantaged groups appeared to capture a deep truth about constitutional equality. The antisubjugation approach also had the virtue (ignored by a current majority of the Supreme Court) of offering an explanation for why race-conscious policies adopted on behalf of subordinated groups ought to be judged by different standards than race-conscious policies that harm subordinated groups.

Fiss's critics have argued that his theory has a difficult time identifying exactly which groups deserve special protection and which do not: the elderly? the disabled? gays and lesbians? the poor? Read too broadly, these critics say, the antisubjugation principle threatens an equality revolution, one that conflates disadvantage with caste, political powerlessness with pariahhood.

The nation is worse off for having largely rejected the application of the antisubjugation principle to African-

Americans. By applying his theory to legal and undocumented immigrants, however, Fiss plays into his critics' hands.

Fiss is surely correct that the federal statutes denying social safety-net benefits to lawful long-term immigrants are immoral and possibly unconstitutional. The Republican congressional majority has recognized how impolitic these policies were by repealing welfare cuts as applied to those immigrants who were residing in the country at the time of the law's enactment. (This reversal, by the way, arguably does significant damage to Fiss's assertion of the political powerlessness of immigrants.)

Fiss finds constitutional fault with the welfare policies because of their "subordinating effect" on immigrants; such laws, he says, run the risk of "transform[ing] immigrants into pariahs." Is he correct? The welfare statutes certainly produce hardship, but, as Fiss recognizes, hardship alone does not establish a constitutional violation: that requires the demonstration of a status-harm— evidence that a historically subordinated group is being kept in its place.

Immigrants as a class (even poor immigrants) are not obvious candidates for Fiss's special protection. Immigrants, unlike African-Americans, can remove themselves from the disadvantaged class; naturalization after five years of lawful residence is fairly straightforward. Furthermore, American immigration policies remain rather generous. As Fiss notes, the United States admits nearly one million legal immigrants a year, and in recent years about the same number of immigrants have naturalized; U.S. immigration and naturalization laws have been shorn of their explicit racial bars; children born to immigrants in the United States are automatically citizens. These are not the kinds of policies usually adopted toward a pariah class. The new welfare law is ugly, targeting those with little political power to object. But these objections apply much more readily to the poor as a class—citizens and immigrants alike—than to immigrants alone.

Additional problems arise with Fiss's description of the scope of his principle. He would not apply his analysis to regulations of immigration—admission and deportation policies—or to the denial of political rights to immigrants. For the former, it is hard to see how the imposition of social disabilities is more "pariah-creating" than laws that threaten deportation. History provides terrible examples of expulsion as a key element in programs of subordination and exploitation.

Fiss would permit the withholding of political rights to immigrants because nations, as voluntary organizations, "require rules of membership" and members are vested with the power to write those rules. He asserts that the imposition of social disabilities, however, is destructive of "the conception of community embodied in the Constitution."

But this distinction seems to assume what it needs to demonstrate. Why are immigrants part of the constitutional community? Why are full members not entitled to provide for the welfare of other full members before looking to the needs of non-members—particularly if the acquisition of full membership is made relatively easy? The answer cannot be that the disfavoring of non-members makes them pariahs. Fiss must say why these groups are entitled to equal treatment in the first place.

The answer, I believe, lies in the antidiscrimination principle that Fiss casts aside. In his hands, that principle does little work, requiring only that the government provide some rational reason for its discrimination—a standard that, as Fiss states, is easily met. But, as he notes later on, violations of the antidiscrimination principle may trigger heightened protection when the classification is one that is viewed as pernicious, likely to be the product of ill will or thoughtlessness, or arbitrary.

It is upon this analysis that I believe the welfare laws denying benefits to immigrants are vulnerable. In the Supreme Court's 1971 decision in *Graham v. Richardson,* barring most forms of *state* discrimination against aliens, Justice Blackmun initially argued that special protection was necessary because immigrants constitute a "discrete and insular minority"—a view that Fiss seems to share. But towards the end of the opinion Blackmun offered another critique of the state law denying welfare to immigrants. Quoting a lower court opinion, he noted that "aliens like citizens pay taxes and may be called into the armed services. . . . [T]hey may live within a state for many years, work in the state and contribute to the economic growth of the state." There can be no "special public interest" [permitting the state to limit benefits to citizens] in tax revenues to which aliens have contributed on an equal basis with the residents of the State.

Blackmun recognized that in the United States immigrants are part of our community and function as such. Their children born here are citizens. They themselves are not pariahs but rather "citizens-in-training." To deny immigrants welfare is to single out for punishment a class that is not appropriately distinguishable from others entitled to welfare.

This reasoning supports the existing constitutional doctrine regarding state discrimination against aliens. Discriminatory federal statutes raise an additional complication. Arguably, the denial of social benefits is no different than an immigration regulation denying admission to persons likely "to become a public charge" (as the immigration laws put it) or requiring that those admitted have sponsors who agree to take care of them in times of need. But a court needn't worry about whether or not these distinctions hold in order to strike down the 1996 welfare law. The current disabilities imposed on immigrants were not exercises of the federal power to regulate immigration in any meaningful sense. Those writing the welfare legislation sought ways to show that welfare "reform" would save money. Terminating benefits to immigrants constituted a significant share of those savings. A court would be justified in seeing the statute for what it is: not a regulation of immigration but rather a regulation of immigrants. Such mistreatment, under the antidiscrimination principle, would require a better governmental justification than merely the desire to cut federal outlays.

So Fiss is correct to be worried about immigrants as easy targets of state and federal lawmakers, particularly when they go looking for ways to save money. But the "pariah" claim seems overstated and unsustainable. It is the class structure of our postindustrial society, far more than our immigration rules, that may be responsible for creating and sustaining a caste of subordinated persons isolated from dominant groups in society.

Caste Recast

ROGERS M. SMITH

Owen Fiss is right to argue that the Equal Protection Clause of the U.S. Constitution should be read to ban not only discrimination but also "the creation of a near-caste structure." He is also right to think that recent anti-immigrant measures pose the danger of contributing to caste-like statuses within the United States. Understandably, he seeks to make an unimpeachable legal case for that conclusion by focusing strictly on the consequences of the disadvantages imposed on immigrants by recent legislative measures.

Fiss's analysis is, however, open to objections that make it far less than a lay-down hand. His case needs to be supplemented by viewing these measures in historical and political perspective. This vantage point makes it clear that what we face now is not the creation of a new caste system but rather the predictable efforts to shore up rotting but still deeply entrenched timbers of our old politically crafted racial and ethnic hierarchies. We pledged ourselves as a nation to eliminate those systems a hundred and thirty years ago. Instead, we have repeatedly protected, even strengthened them. Given those realities, we should see it as constitutionally appropriate for courts, lawmakers, and citizens to concern themselves with challenging government actions that work to preserve, or even enhance, the caste systems intertwining color and class that have loomed so large and for so long in American life.

The heart of Fiss's case is summed up in the sentence "We ought not to subjugate immigrants, not because we owe them anything, but to preserve our society as a community of equals." That appealing argument is open to two major objections, both of which Fiss addresses, but not decisively.

The first objection is that it makes no sense in this context to say that we must "preserve" America as a "community of *equals* [emphasis mine]," because even legal immigrants have never been fully equal members of the U.S. political community, and not even Fiss thinks they should be. He does not think they should vote. He says it makes sense to confine voting to those who have professed loyalty to the political principles that voters are supposed to sustain and extend, and that immigrants have relatively easy access to that status via naturalization. But precisely because immigrants do have easy access to citizenship and voting, many might say that resident aliens who forego naturalization have indicated that they do not accept equal responsibility for the fate of the American republic. Hence, arguably, they cannot claim equal benefits as a matter of right. As they could get both citizenship and full benefits if they wanted, but have chosen not to do so, their deprivation appears to be their choice. Undocumented aliens, in contrast, cannot choose to become citizens, and so they might more plausibly be seen as having a status that was merely the best among dreadful alternatives—not the product of meaningfully free choices.

The second objection, however, is that it makes no sense to say that we must preserve our "*community* of equals [emphasis again mine]" when we are discussing undocumented immigrants, who are not legally part of the American "community" at all. If, as Fiss says, "the very existence of the nation as a community" rests in its power "to determine its own membership," then this lack of legal membership in the American community seems decisive. Whether undocumented aliens are subjugated or not appears irrelevant to maintaining equality *within* the community. If subjugating them remains wrong, then spending resources to return them to their countries of origin may seem at least as obvious a course as spending resources to aid their continued presence in the United States.

Fiss responds the same way to both of these possibilities—he claims that legal immigrants may choose not to take citizenship despite loss of benefits, and that some immigrants may choose to come to this country without legal permission to do so. The Constitution, he says, forbids "even voluntary subjugation" because this "would disfigure society." Here he overstates. The Thirteenth Amendment forbids only "involuntary servitude." It is true that we understand this ban to prohibit people from selling themselves into chattel slavery, but only because most of us believe that such an act can never be a truly free choice. It is far less certain that people who remain resident aliens without benefits when citizenship is available to them are really in the thralls of any such "involuntary servitude." And even in regard to those with undocumented status, reasonable people can disagree over whether this represents a free choice or not.

Fiss can probably defend his position further. Still, these problems are enough to justify pursuing his conclusion by a different route. Fiss is right to judge statutes by their consequences, but those consequences should be appraised in light of the broader historical contexts in which statutes arise and are implemented. We should recall that up until 1965, U.S. citizenship laws visibly defined an elaborate racial and ethnic caste system. The national origins quota system, enacted explicitly to limit the access of the "lower races" to U.S. citizenship, prevailed until the federal Immigration Act of 1965. Numerous state and local measures explicitly aimed at disfranchising African-Americans in the South and many Latinos in the Southwest also remained effective until the 1965 Voting Rights Act. Racially and ethnically based denials of access to full U.S. citizenship thus operated against most of the people of color within and outside the borders of the United States up to a generation ago.

It is painful to recognize that the United States was so recently a caste society, but that is the reality. It was, to be sure, always a contested reality: hence the thin veil of "separate but equal" for the Jim Crow system of disfranchisement and subordination. The cumulative results of those contests have produced great and enduring gains for the nation's racial and ethnic minorities. We must also recognize, however, that every period of racially egalitarian reforms in American life has been followed by a backlash in which progress ceased and some systems of racial inequality were reestablished in modified form. For example, blacks in North Carolina gained the vote after the American Revolution, then lost it in the 1830s, regained it during Reconstruction, then effectively lost it in the 1890s, regaining it again only after 1965. The Civil War and Reconstruction periods also saw federal efforts to encourage immigration and relax racial restrictions on naturalization, but with the end of Reconstruction new race-based immigration restrictions spread.

Though backlash is not the whole story, it is impossible to deny that today the movement against immigrants in part expresses opposition to the results of the civil rights and immigration reforms of the 1960s. In 1992, and more elaborately in 1995, *Forbes* and *National Review* editor Peter Brimelow lamented that the 1965 immigration reforms threatened the traditional "racial hegemony of white Americans" in the United States and also added new "colored" beneficiaries of affirmative action.[1] In 1994, Richard Herrnstein and Charles Murray's book *The Bell Curve* complained that "Latino and black" immigration was lowering American intelligence and providing new beneficiaries for America's allegedly counterproductive welfare, antidiscrimination, and affirmative action laws.[2] Then came the anti-immigrant Proposition 187 in California, followed by the state's Proposition 209, ending affirmative action there, and the 1996 welfare reform act, which cut off benefits to immigrants, identified in the popular mind primarily with Mexicans, Haitians, and other often impoverished people of color. These are people the United States had long excluded and/or subjugated by law; they are the people already much reviled under the label "underclass," and they are the people most hurt by recent anti-immigrant and anti-welfare laws. Seen in historical and political perspective, then, these measures appear to simply reestablish certain all-too-familiar American caste systems.

I believe the Fourteenth Amendment is a constitutional mandate for American governments to make sure their policies are not perpetuating these old caste systems, but rather are working to alleviate them and their effects: to achieve equal protection for all. Because recent laws do the reverse, I agree with Fiss that courts should invalidate them. I also recognize, however, that courts may be reluctant to rely so much on history and sur-rounding contemporary circumstances in assessing the consequences of recent legislation. But if those problems mean that efforts to repudiate these laws by judicial means may not work, then American citizens have all the more reason to take action themselves to reject these measures and all others that threaten to extend the cruel legacies of our racist past.

Let Them Vote

JENNIFER GORDON

I share Owen Fiss's concern about legislation denying immigrants basic benefits, but I propose a different solution. Almost all the disabilities that concern Fiss are imposed by the states. Why not simply let non-citizen immigrants vote in state and local elections?[1]

Contrary to popular understanding, the law imposes no impediment to non-citizen voting in the United States, even on the federal level. The Constitution does not require that voters be citizens; the decision about who can vote in federal elections rests in the hands of each state. During the eighteenth and nineteenth centuries, at least twenty-two U.S. states and territories enfranchised immigrants in both state and federal elections; non-citizens voted in the United States as recently as 1928. In the case of *Minor v. Wisdom* (1874), the Supreme Court approvingly noted that "citizenship has not in all cases been made a condition precedent to the enjoyment of the right of suffrage," citing Missouri, Texas, Indiana, Georgia, Alabama, Arkansas, Florida, Kansas, and Minnesota as examples of states then allowing non-naturalized immigrants to vote. Offering the franchise was a way of attracting new settlers to a vast and under-populated country.

This is not 1874, and the United States is not looking to encourage more immigration. Today, Takoma Park, Maryland, stands as the only local government in the United States that has enfranchised non-citizens. But as the Maastricht Treaty acknowledged with its grant to all Europeans of the right to vote in European countries other than their own, and as Norway, Sweden, Denmark, and the Netherlands have long realized, a forceful case can be made that non-citizen immigrants, and even undocumented people (so-called illegal aliens) should be allowed to vote in local elections.

The most fundamental argument for this proposition is founded on a basic democratic principle: that a community should only be able to bind members by its laws—and require their support through taxes—if it allows them to participate in its politics. This principle condemns efforts to build a democratic political community by excluding non-citizens and implies instead that the right to participate by voting should rest on an individual's stake in the community and her or his interest in the outcome, not on whether she or he has taken the citizenship test. I believe that states and local governments already treat non-citizens—both legal permanent residents and undocumented people—sufficiently like community members to qualify them as voters under this conception of voting rights.

For example, all resident non-citizens must pay income taxes regardless of their immigration status. Contrary to popular belief, most undocumented people do not "freeload" on the system, consuming services while paying no taxes. In this country, immigration laws require proof of tax payment for the five years previous to becoming legal; as a result, many undocumented immigrants go out of their way to pay taxes, often without receiving the refund to which they are entitled because these payments are made under false Social Security numbers.

Moreover, non-citizens participate in community life in many other ways. As Fiss points out, the Supreme Court guaranteed the right of undocumented children to attend public school in *Plyler v. Doe*. (Both New York City and Chicago have recognized this by allowing all parents to vote in school board elections and to hold school board offices regardless of their immigration status.) In similar ways, non-citizens use and support police, sanitation, and other city and state services. Their dollars—by the millions—support private services and businesses as well. And they are bound by the laws of local, state, and federal governments.

Lots of people have trouble accepting this argument because of their misperceptions about the life of undocumented persons: they cannot imagine that such immigrants are active participants in a community. Fiss's bleak description of people who are forced "to survive by begging or stealing and thus to live at the margins of society and to prey on it" is a classic example. Having worked with such immigrants for fourteen years, I can unequivocally state they do not live this kind of feral and reclusive existence; instead, they participate vigorously in the economy (albeit often underground), and in the churches, schools, and communities in which they live. Unless forced to dig into their wallets for their immigration papers, they are often indistinguishable from any other member of the community, and their interest and stake in the community's political decisions is as strong as that of any citizen.

There is no shortage of counterarguments to the principle that this stake should guarantee immigrants the vote. (Fiss himself mentions two.)

1. Non-citizens have not sworn a loyalty oath to the United States, and therefore can not be trusted to vote in the best interests of this country, as opposed to their own interests or those of their country of origin. Proponents of this argument ignore the fact that people born in the United States are not required to swear allegiance to the Constitution. We assume that by virtue of their birth on these shores they will be "loyal" voters. If birth is a sufficient proxy for loyalty, why is the active choice to move to this country not an even stronger proof of commitment to our values? In addition, state and local elections offer the voter little or no opportunity for treason. Both immigration and foreign policy are decided exclusively by the federal government.

2. Immigrants as a group would tip the political balance in a state or community by voting in their own interest. Noncitizens could, for example, vote to grant state public assistance to undocumented people, to make the local community a "sanctuary city" for refugees, or to have bilingual instruction in the public schools. While it may be true that non-citizen immigrants would vote for these things, it is no less true that citizens vote in their own interests all the time—property owners about property taxes, parents about schools, etc. In *Carrington v. Rash*, a 1964 case about the right of soldiers temporarily stationed in Texas to vote in that state, the Supreme Court unequivocally held that " '[f]encing out' from the franchise a sector of the population because of the way they may vote is constitutionally impermissible."

3. If a non-citizen wanted to vote, he or she could easily become a citizen. Sadly, this is no longer true. Yes, immigrants who are legal permanent residents (with green cards) are eligible to become citizens after five years—if they can wade through the two-million-person, two-year backlog. But many immigrants, including hundreds of thousands of legal immigrants here with temporary work permits, do not have green cards. They live and work in communities all over the United States, but for most of them naturalization is not an option. This means that many of the people that Fiss is concerned about do not have the choice to become voters, now or ever.

4. Non-citizen immigrants might return to another country, voluntarily or through deportation; as transients, they should not be allowed to vote. Immigrants should be subjected to the same proof-of-residency requirements for voting in state and local elections as citizens. Just as U.S. citizens can vote in the state where they have made a home, even though tomorrow they may move, non-citizens should be able to vote where they reside, even though there is a chance that they will someday leave. Again, the Supreme Court's decision in the case of the soldiers stationed in Texas provides guidance. Texas had denied these soldiers the right to vote in part because their frequent transfers turned them into transients. The Court found that it was not legitimate for the state to decide for a group of people as a class that their status rendered them transient, without giving the individuals a chance to prove the bona fides of their residence.

5. If we let non-citizens vote, we will erase the last meaningful distinction between "us" and "them." Not true. The right to vote in federal elections would remain exclusively the province of citizens, as would the right to hold federal office. Non-citizen immigrants could still be deported, and would be subjected to immigration laws and restrictions in general. It is unlikely that non-citizens would be in the majority in the bulk of voting districts; therefore, states and localities are also likely to continue imposing some distinctions between citizens and non-citizens.

6. Non-citizen immigrants are too ignorant of U.S. government structure, politics, and culture to vote responsibly. Unfortunately, it is no less true that many United States–born citizens are too ignorant of U.S. government structure, politics, and culture to vote responsibly. The Supreme Court's observations in another voting rights case, in which a state had imposed durational residency requirements on newcomers before they could vote, are equally apposite here:

The classifications created by durational residency requirements obviously permit any longtime resident to vote regardless of his knowledge of the issues—and obviously many longtime residents do not have any. On the other hand, the classifications bar from the franchise many other, admittedly new, residents who have become at least minimally, and often fully informed about the issues. Indeed, recent migrants who take the time to register and vote shortly after moving tend to be those . . . who make it a point to be informed and knowledgeable about the issues. (*Dunn v. Blumstein*, 405 U.S. 330 (1972) at 358.)

Because non-citizens have chosen this country rather than having been born into it and are in the process of learning about its language and culture, they often pay more attention to the events around them than jaded citizens do. Foreign-language television, radio, and newspapers in most immigrant communities keep people up to date on politics here as well as abroad. As the measures protective of linguistic minorities in the Voting Rights Amendments of 1975 indicate, we should not assume that voters who do not speak English will vote any less intelligently than those who do. It is also important to realize that not all non-citizens will register to vote; only those most interested and aware will do so. And undocumented people will only register if they are willing to take the risk of having their names published in public voting rolls, which will deter all but the most politically active from participating.

7. Allowing non-citizen voting would increase fraud. Although this is frequently claimed, I can not understand why the votes of non-citizens are any more likely to be bought or sold than the votes of citizens: immigration status does not seem to be an adequate proxy for dishonesty, never mind a compelling one. In any case, states can and should address this concern through anti-fraud measures applied equally to all voters regardless of their citizenship status.

To conclude, let me be clear about the politics of my argument. I do not expect the Supreme Court to require the enfranchisement of non-citizens. But if a particular state or community were to be convinced by the arguments put forth above and decide to extend the vote to immigrants, I think the Court might well uphold such

a decision. The Constitution permits such an arrange-
ment, and courts have frequently upheld local laws
granting nonresidents with sufficient interest in local issues (as evidenced most often by property holdings) the
right to vote in local elections.

It is not an easy thing to change an idea so deeply in-
grained as the concept that voting is the exclusive province of citizens. Nevertheless, a closer look at state and
local communities, and the lives of non-citizen residents
within them—as well as the effects to date of disenfran-
chisement—supports the idea of non-citizen suffrage as
a fair and rational solution to the concerns that so many
of us share with Owen Fiss.

A Right to Dignity

ULRICH PREUSS

$\mathcal{N}$owadays it is hard to find a country that is favorable to immigration. In affluent countries, many of which are plagued by mass unemployment, heavy strains upon the basic institutions of the welfare state, and uncertain economic prospects, immigration is widely viewed as an economic burden. Not surprisingly, the member states of the European Union make many efforts to discourage legal and illegal immigration and to make the sojourn of those who have not been dissuaded as unpleasant as possible. Given their character as constitutional states and their commitment to basic human rights, these countries do, of course, seek to maintain a minimum standard of human existence below which nobody should fall. This standard seems to be quite malleable. Owen Fiss's argument on these questions is a welcome opportunity to compare different constitutional approaches to the problem.

Take, for example, Germany, a country which after World War II established a tradition of hospitality towards refugees and victims of political persecution, but which does not provide legal means of "normal" immigration. Naturalization is a matter of administrative discretion and does not involve large numbers of people. What Fiss calls "political disability"—the exclusion of aliens from political participation, particularly from the right to vote—implies the definition of the nation as a "community of citizens"; yet, according to the currently predominant (albeit increasingly challenged) theories of the state and of democracy, there is no citizenship without nationality. Hence aliens cannot be citizens.

Rather than delving into this question, I would like to turn to what Fiss calls "social disability." Here I leave aside the category of permanent legal alien resident— largely the "guest workers" of the 1960s and 1970s and their families—because in Germany they are by and large fairly well integrated and no longer live at the margins of society. This, however, is not the case with all other kinds of immigrants, be they refugees from countries ridden by war or civil war, asylum-seekers, or illegal labor immigrants. Obviously the situation of illegal immigrants is the worst. They live in a state of complete lawlessness because they cannot even claim the rights due them from their (illegal) labor contracts with their employers without revealing their illegal residence and being immediately deported. Thus it has frequently happened that employers of illegal workers pay wages far below the standard and inform or threaten to inform the police about the immigrants' illegal status. These immigrants are exposed to all kinds of blackmail and live in a shadowy world outside civilized society. In comparison to them, the legal immigrants—asylum-seekers and refugees—are of course in a better situation because they are recognized as persons with legal capacity. But this does not mean that they have a share in the benefits of the larger society. For instance, asylum-seekers are excluded from the right to freedom of movement, to work, or to live in a private home; indeed, they are usually forced to live in camps. Moreover, their material standard of living has been continuously declining, and the government's most recent measure (July 1998) has deprived them even of the right to appropriate medical care. Undoubtedly social disability is imposed on them.

Interestingly, neither of the two constitutional arguments examined by Fiss, which could potentially protect immigrants from social disability, can be applied to the situation in Germany. Although it is stated in Article 3 Paragraph 3 of the Basic Law that no person shall suffer prejudice because of (among other things) birth, race, language, or national origin, it is still possible for aliens to have fewer rights than Germans since the constitution itself makes a distinction between basic rights, which are only accessible to Germans, and universally applicable rights. Moreover, discrimination is justified in Germany on grounds similar to those invoked in American constitutional doctrine. It can be claimed that if the smaller allotment of social benefits to immigrants is a necessary and appropriate means for the realization of a legitimate social purpose, then Article 3 Paragraph 3 is not violated.

By contrast, it would be quite difficult to make use of Fiss's central argument in German constitutional discourse. The claim that a law is unconstitutional if it transforms immigrants into pariahs, that is, if it creates "a social structure that is inconsistent with the conception of community embodied in the Constitution" is essentially consequentialist. It presupposes an idea or vision of a society that is incompatible with certain circumstances, such as the existence of a pariah-like population. Constitutional lawyers and the courts have to realize or to redesign this vision and determine whether the current state of affairs is compatible with it or not. This is, of course, a difficult undertaking because both constitutional lawyers and individual courts may disagree about the societal ideals enshrined in the constitution, more so than about the question of what a particular constitutional right may require for a particular claimant.

More crucially, Fiss's approach may lead the court in a particular case to the judgment that the act or omission under scrutiny does not lead to a social structure that violates the constitutional concept of a "good society," much as it may violate essential human needs. In other words, the protection of the neediest who have to strive for their status as members of the larger society may be accomplished more appropriately and more efficiently through categorical rather than consequentialist arguments. The standard of "social disability" can be construed as relative, depending upon the overall picture that the constitution draws of society according to the divergent interpretations of constitutional lawyers and courts. If, instead, we accept the criterion of human dignity, the space for divergent interpretations of the responsibilities that society has to fulfill is much narrower. To be sure, it still exists; the subjection of German legislation to the almost sacramental protection of human dignity articulated in Article 1 of the Basic Law gives sufficient evidence of this condition. The public debate in Germany about the reasonable standard of living that must not be denied even to illegal immigrants clearly shows that the categorical concept of human dignity is malleable. Still, I think that Fiss's functional approach leaves more room for opportunistic interpretations of the constitution than would a standard that grounds society's responsibilities towards immigrants in an individual right.

A final remark: From the point of view of German constitutional law, Fiss's assumption that the judiciary is the appropriate institution of corrective justice is not plausible. In the European continental tradition, the primary protection of the individual rests with the parliament. If, as is certainly the case, the parliament cannot be regarded as the locus of either actual or virtual representation of immigrants, the latter's last resort is the courts. But in the German tradition the courts are not supposed to correct society's structural deficiencies. They protect individuals against a wrong and prejudiced application of the law, not against wrong and prejudiced laws themselves.

Beyond Borders

IRIS M. YOUNG

*D*oes anyone *deserve* to be a pariah? Many supporters of laws forbidding the employment of illegal immigrants or denying them public benefits would say yes. They would say that people who sneak across borders with the aim of taking advantage of the benefits they might find on the other side deserve to live more miserable lives than their fellow nationals legally admitted to the same territory. Illegal immigrants deserve their pariah status, in this view, not because they are immigrants but because they have broken the law. Owen Fiss argues that the Constitution does not support such reasoning. As long as immigrants are here, whether or not they are here legally, an antisubordination principle following from the Equal Protection Clause implies that no person can be treated differently with regard to access to social benefits or economic opportunities.

I agree generally with Fiss's humanist sentiments. I also applaud his use of the principle of antisubordination rather than a principle of nondiscrimination to adjudicate group-based legal classifications. Despite my general agreement with Fiss's conclusion and his approach, however, I do not think he has convincingly shown that the principle of antisubordination should apply to illegal immigrants in the same way that it applies to everyone else residing in the sovereign territory of the United States.

There is a proper difference, Fiss says, between being a member of the political community and being a member of society. While it is legitimate to set certain conditions of language, learning, and loyalty on political rights, Fiss suggests, social membership itself confers social rights. Members of our society, whether citizens or not, cannot be made to suffer state-imposed social disabilities. When the state explicitly admits immigrants, they are admitted, one might even say welcomed, into society. As members of the society the Constitution governs, they cannot be made into social pariahs. Thus the antisubordination principle applies to legal immigrants as well as to citizens.

For this argument to apply in the same way to illegal and legal immigrants alike, Fiss must be saying that illegal immigrants are also members of our society. Indeed he does seem to think this. We ought not to subjugate illegal immigrants, he says, because we want to preserve our society as a community of equals; subordinating illegal immigrants creates a social structure inconsistent with that community. But what, for Fiss, has made illegal immigrants into members of this society to whom an antisubordination principle applies? I do not see that Fiss answers this key question.

The question is crucial because the idea that illegal aliens are members of society is precisely what supporters of laws against affording them employment opportunities or social benefits deny. Those supporters would agree that legal immigrants have been admitted to the society, but deny that the same is true of illegal immigrants. We have a right to deport illegal immigrants, then, simply because they are not members of our society, and for the same reason we have a right to deny them social benefits.

Fiss suggests that merely being within the territory of the United States is sufficient to make illegal immigrants members of the society. But surely this is arbitrary. How can it be that one day a person is not a member of the society because he is in Tijuana, but when he has arrived in San Diego he is a member? Surely crossing the borders of a sovereign state does not itself make one a member of its society. Opponents of social benefits for illegal immigrants agree. These are not social members but alien invaders. Writing social disabilities for them into law does not create a pariah status for them, in this view; it merely recognizes their status as alien invaders.

As I said above, I agree with Fiss's policy objectives. I agree that it is wrong for the states of Texas or California actively to deny opportunities and benefits to illegal residents of those states. With Fiss I think that this is wrong primarily because the legal residents of Texas or California are socially connected to the illegal residents, and by extension all those in the territory of the United States may be so connected. These social connections are not founded in the immigrant's presence in legally bounded sovereign territory, however. Rather, they are founded in the cultural, economic, familial, environmental, and communicative movements and interactions across the mountains of the Southwest, or indeed across the Pacific Ocean. Citizens of Mexico or Honduras show up in Los Angeles or San Antonio because they are already connected to those places—they have been illegally recruited for jobs, or they have friends and family there; they have traveled there with a group, or they have seen the gringos coming over the border to pay one-tenth the wages they pay in California or to buy cheap goods under the protection of local police. The social and economic connections between people in Mexico and Central America and the Southwestern United States are wide and dense, arguably denser than my connection with either region as I sit here in Pittsburgh. A sovereign legal border does little to obstruct those connections. The same may be said for the social and economic connections between Shanghai and San Francisco or Manila and Minneapolis.

My point is that the social and economic connections that ground rights and obligations between people are not confined by sovereign state borders. We are in a continuous society with other people when actions and institutions of production, distribution, and communication, among others, connect us so tightly that what some of us do in one country is likely to affect the lives of people in another and vice versa. Those who live within the sovereign borders of the United States are socially connected in these ways to many outsiders. The policies and actions of powerful public and private institutions of the United States affect the lives of millions elsewhere, often to their detriment and our relative benefit. It is because we are already socially connected to these outsiders in myriad ways that it is wrong, when they come here, for us to use the law to deny them benefits that others enjoy, especially when they have done no harm other than to have sought a better life. Since here the social connections do not correspond to political jurisdiction, however, I wonder whether the Constitution really can protect the moral rights of illegal as well as legal immigrants. Those who wish to work for transnational justice may do better to rely on and help construct more transnational legal institutions.

A Moral Responsibility

Owen Fiss is right to encourage us to doubt the consti-
tutionality of both state laws and provisions of the 1996
Welfare Reform Act that deny illegal and legal immigrants what might be called "social welfare goods"—access to medical care, education, food stamps, and job opportunities. He is also correct, in my view, to suggest that
the unconstitutionality of these provisions follows from
their inherent tendency to subjugate a group of people by
forcing them into pariah or near-pariah status, rather
than from than their tendency to group individuals un-
fairly according to an irrational classification. As Fiss argues, the Equal Protection Clause, best read, does indeed prohibit the severe subjugation of groups of persons
no less than it prohibits the unfair classification of individuals. Further, and although this "antisubjugation
interpretation" of the Equal Protection Clause has been
only a minor theme in the U.S. Supreme Court's development of the Fourteenth Amendment (in contrast to
the antidiscrimination principle), Fiss is probably right
to suggest that the antisubjugation principle may rest on

a superior reading of the clause than the antidiscrimination principle. The antisubjugation principle, for which Fiss and many others now argue, may as a general matter represent an ideal that is truer to the amendment's history, closer to the natural reading of the language of the clause, and more conducive to justice than the cramped antidiscrimination principle the Court now embraces. But whether or not that's the case, Fiss is surely right to conclude that if we read the Equal Protection Clause as prohibiting the subjugation of groups of people by imposing pariah status upon them, then the provisions of the 1996 Welfare Reform Act denying immigrants access to basic welfare and social goods are unconstitutional. Fiss's interpretation of the clause, and his argument for its application to the laws governing immigrants, is an unorthodox, even dissident reading. The result is not one that the Court is ever likely to reach, at least not on the grounds Fiss advocates. Nevertheless, both the interpretation and the result are in my view correct.

Where Fiss goes wrong, I believe, is in coupling this reading of the Fourteenth Amendment with the utterly conventional and orthodox view expressed at the end of his article, to the effect that it is and should be the role of the judiciary to police this constitutional antisubjugation principle against the errors of the political branches of government. In Fiss's view, shared by virtually all liberal constitutional scholars, the majority, through its representatives, acts in response to political pressures, and the Court, through the justices, acts so as to ensure that the political will of the people results in laws that are in accordance with the communitarianism, egalitarianism, and general conception of justice at the heart of our constitutional scheme of government. The legislative role is to enact the people's will, while the Court's job is to ensure that we "preserve our society as a community of equals," as envisioned and even mandated by the Constitution.

There are serious problems with this division of constitutional labor, even from the perspective of one who wholeheartedly shares Fiss's egalitarian commitments. The first is obvious and strategic: there is next to no chance that the Court will adopt a view of the Fourteenth Amendment that bears even a family resemblance to the one Fiss advocates. The second is legal, or textual: by its own terms, the Fourteenth Amendment's Section 5 envisions congressional rather than judicial enforcement of its promises. A third and deeper problem, however, and the one least often noted, is at once moral and political. It is a problem that has been evident since the beginning of our practice of judicial review but tends to be buried with each new wave of righteous, justice-based litigation brought under the majestic clauses of the Fourteenth Amendment—and even more deeply buried when the proposed litigation promises some measure of success. Fiss's argument—that the U.S. Supreme Court should invalidate scores of state and federal laws impeding immigrants' access to social goods on the grounds, basically, of the inegalitarianism of these laws—indirectly highlights what the moral costs of its success might be.

By delegating to the Court the work of ensuring compliance with constitutional norms, Fiss effectively divests the people and their representatives of their own constitutional obligations and responsibilities: we can be constitutionally reckless, he seems to be saying, if the Court is vigilant. To be sure, this divestiture would hardly matter if the Constitution were nothing but a string of procedural, structural, nuts-and-bolts legalistic regulations. And it would matter even less if the Constitution were merely a tool of the propertied classes, as is sometimes claimed. But these constrained conceptions do not accord with the Constitution as Fiss and his fellow liberal constitutionalists read it. For them, the Constitution is the expression and embodiment of our egalitarian and communitarian better selves: it presents and imposes our defining conception of social justice— at once liberal and egalitarian, respectful of individuals and mindful of our communitarian natures—and it embodies, expresses, and enforces our political morality. Yet Fiss, in his focus on the Court's constitutional responsibility, overlooks the people's responsibility for moral governance. His implicit message seems to be that our politics need not be constrained by moral ideals, aspirations, or conceptions of justice, so long as our higher law and the Court that interprets it are.

There is something deeply wrong—and, I submit, deeply illiberal—about this conception of politics. Our politics, and not just our law, should be informed by a moral responsibility not to create pariahs or allow a permanent underclass to develop, or to permit a situation in which lower castes live among us. It may be, as Fiss insists, the role of the apolitical Court, acting "above the political fray," to ensure that "the majority" does not unduly subjugate an already downtrodden group of people. But if the legal imperative for this moral constraint stems from the Constitution, and especially from the Fourteenth Amendment (which directs Congress, not the courts, to enact laws ensuring compliance with its grand promises), then it is imperative that the majority and their representatives, acting *in* the fray, come to an appreciation of the moral and constitutional constraints upon them. If the Constitution says what Fiss thinks it says (and I believe it does) then the audience for his interpretive argument must be the people, not the courts.

Liberal constitutionalists perversely insist on a division of labor that imagines the Court as societal superego, voice of reason, or moral conscience, whose peculiar job it is to constrain an out-of-control majoritarian political process motivated by irrational and often hateful passions. We should worry that this very image might undercut rather than bolster the slim chance that our political lives and choices might one day be informed by the very egalitarian and communitarian commitments that Owen Fiss, to his great credit, so clearly holds.

Open Borders

MARK TUSHNET

Owen Fiss's proposal doesn't go far enough. He as-
sumes that an immigration policy founded on creating
legal barriers to people's entry into this country is just.
But the long-term goal of immigration policy should be
open borders and fairly easy naturalization, with social
welfare benefits denied to people from the time they arrive until the time they decide to become citizens. Such
a policy is more consistent with the American people's
historical aspirations. The United States is a nation
founded, as Lincoln said, upon propositions of political
theory articulated in the Declaration of Independence.
All who accept those propositions should be welcomed
as members of the American polity.

Fiss agrees that we can deny *membership* goods, such
as the right to vote, to long-term lawfully resident aliens.
But, he suggests, we should not deny them *social welfare*
goods, because such denials create conditions for a permanent caste of second-class residents who will be subject to exploitation because they cannot rely on the rem-
nants of the welfare state's safety-net programs.

But long-term lawfully resident aliens don't risk becoming pariahs by law. Federal law makes it pretty easy for them to become citizens. They don't have membership or social welfare goods because they are, as Annette Baier puts it, "voluntary aliens." Baier argues that some benefits flow from being a voluntary alien. Such an individual can maintain an ambivalent relation to the United States, with some investment in its culture because of long-term residency but some distance because he or she isn't a U.S. citizen.[1]

For Baier, sustaining that ambivalence requires that the voluntary alien be denied *some* things, and she thinks that some social welfare goods might be among them. The very nature of *voluntary* alienage matters in another way. It's hard to see how denying voluntary aliens social welfare goods creates a risk that they would form a permanent caste vulnerable to exploitation. After all, they can change their status when they want. The mere possibility of their doing so sharply reduces the risk that they would form a subordinated caste.

Illegal entrants aside, the risk that Fiss worries about involves only lawfully present aliens from the time of their arrival until they become eligible for citizenship. And, again, precisely because there is a time limit on the problem, we can't create a caste out of that group either.

(Of course, all this rests on the proposition that it's fairly easy for a lawfully present long-term resident alien to become a citizen. That's largely true as a matter of law, less so as a matter of practice. But we could improve the practice without worrying about any large questions of principle.)

The real problem, of course, is posed by the situation of aliens who arrive in the United States illegally. Here Fiss's proposal has real bite. But its incentive effects, which he notes in passing, are clearly in tension with the proposition—which Fiss accepts—that the United States can restrict entry. In effect, Fiss says to people outside the United States, "We're going to use guns and soldiers to keep you out, and we're going to throw you out if you get here and we find you. But if you manage to get here and as long as we don't find you, you'll get access not only to the general market opportunities available in the United States but to our social welfare goods too."

In response to concerns about incentives for illegal immigration, Fiss says in effect that the only way to discourage unlawful entry is by force—force at the point of entry and force through deportation. I suspect that Fiss's analysis is driven by Justice Brennan's opinion in *Plyler*. We know, Brennan said, in effect, that we're not going to use enough force to control the borders or deport people who enter unlawfully. And *that* really does mean that we risk creating a pariah caste.

But we can respond in two ways to the problem of our practical unwillingness to keep or throw people out. As Fiss says, we can admit to ourselves that they are going to be here and decide to keep them from becoming a pariah caste by ensuring that they receive social welfare goods.

Or we could decide that we are wrong in trying to keep them out.

Usually people defend restrictive immigration policies on two grounds. The first is pragmatic: there'd be a flood of purely economic immigrants, attracted to the United States only by the huge differences between their economic opportunities at home and those that exist here. Frankly, I don't see what's so terrible about that. In equilibrium, everybody's going to be better off. But I'm sure that the transition to an equilibrium would be extremely disruptive, so I'm willing to accept a gradual relaxation of entry restrictions rather than their immediate abolition.

The second ground offered for restrictive policies is more principled. As Fiss puts it, distinguishing between aliens and citizens (which he mistakenly thinks is the same as distinguishing between legal and illegal immigrants) is "essential to the very existence of the nation as a community." An open-borders policy would eliminate our distinctive national character (whatever that is).

Readers of *Boston Review* have already been exposed to a substantial debate about nationalism's merits,[2] which I don't want to repeat here, but it's worth pointing out that we can accept the fundamental idea of nationalism while proposing an open borders policy too. It all depends on *what* the nation's character is. There's a strong tradition in the United States that holds that we are a nation committed to a set of universal values accessible to reason (that's my translation of the opening of the Declaration of Independence). That's what we ask about when people become naturalized citizens. And it's a pretty attractive vision of national character.

In short, what's best about the United States would be preserved by a policy of open borders and naturalization available to anyone who agreed with the fundamental principles that animate our polity. The second element of this policy is already in place. It's time to think seriously about the first.

Messy Realities

MYRON WEINER

The legal and moral argument put forth by Owen Fiss—that all foreigners in the United States are entitled to the same opportunities as citizens for employment, education, Medicare, Medicaid, public housing, food stamps, and other social benefits—fails to consider why we make distinctions among different categories of foreign residents and the varied public purposes that these distinctions serve. Twenty-five million individuals are admitted into the United States each year, the vast majority of them for a limited duration. Twenty-three million are temporary visitors, that is, tourists and business travelers; 430,000 are students, their spouses and children; 227,000 are temporary workers; and 215,000 are exchange visitors. In addition, the United States admits about 750,000 people as immigrants each year and another 140,000 or so as refugees. A complex set of rules governs the rights and benefits granted to each of the categories of persons entering the country.

U.S. law distinguishes between immigrants and refugees admitted for permanent residence, and non-immigrants who are admitted for limited time periods for purposes such as tourism, study, or temporary work. Temporary visitors are barred from permanent employment and social benefits. Foreign students may work, but are not entitled to most public benefits. Temporary workers may receive some public benefits and their employers are legally required to provide others. Except for legal immigrants and refugees, visitors do not have the right to remain indefinitely, though complex government regulations enable students and other short-term visitors to seek a change in their status in order to become immigrants. Legal immigrants are given access to public benefits that approximate those of citizens, but pending their admission to citizenship there are some restrictions on this access. Illegal immigrants are denied most benefits, although their children may attend school—restrictive efforts in California notwithstanding—and they have access to emergency care in hospitals.

The rights and benefits of individuals who reside in the United States but are not citizens are subject to debate. The issue was initially raised in Texas when a local school board sought to bar school admission to children of illegal aliens, a decision subsequently overruled by the Supreme Court in *Plyler v. Doe* in 1982. In 1994, California voters adopted Proposition 187, which denied educational and other benefits to illegal immigrants, and in 1996 Congress passed new welfare legislation that restricted legal immigrants from acquiring most welfare benefits. In mid-1998, Congress amended this legislation by reinstating food stamps to a quarter of a million children, elderly, and handicapped immigrants if they had entered the United States before August 1996, when the welfare reform legislation took effect; Congress also agreed to restore Medicaid and Supplemental Security Income (SSI) benefits to 420,000 legal immigrants who had lost these benefits because of the 1996 welfare reform legislation.

The debate over benefits is partly driven by fiscal considerations. State and local governments bear most of the cost of public services provided to legal and illegal immigrants and their children, while most of the taxes that immigrants pay go to the federal government. The debate is also driven by a desire to distinguish between immigrants admitted lawfully and illegal immigrants. Many U.S. citizens feel strongly that illegal immigrants should not receive public assistance other than emergency medical attention. There is also a debate about which categories of social benefits should be provided to legal immigrants. Sponsors of newly arrived immigrants are expected to assume financial responsibility for those who otherwise might become a public charge. Many members of Congress, for example, argue that elderly immigrant parents should be supported by their children and should not be eligible for SSI benefits until they are citizens or have been in the United States for a specified period.

Whether immigrants, legal or illegal, are entitled to

the same rights and benefits as those granted to citizens is an issue in all advanced industrial societies. Or, to put the question another way, should citizens have rights and benefits that are greater than those of non-citizens? Is the welfare state intended only for citizens of a country or for all who reside within its territory? Fiss argues that there should be no distinctions between citizens and non-citizens with respect to social benefits and access to employment. Citizens have the exclusive right to vote, but they should have no exclusive claim to any other rights or social benefits. Nor, he argues, should any distinctions be made among categories of immigrants. Illegal residents should be entitled to education, social welfare benefits, and the right to employment no less than legal immigrants. "Laws that bar illegal immigrants from working," he writes, ". . . force illegal immigrants to survive by begging or stealing and thus to live at the margins of society."

Fiss rests his argument on constitutional and on moral grounds. Though I defer to his superior expertise on constitutional questions, I note that thus far the courts have not endorsed his position that the Fourteenth Amendment prevents legislative bodies from drawing distinctions between citizens and non-citizens or between legal and illegal residents. *Plyler*, which overruled the Texas restrictions on school admission for illegal migrants' children, was, as he notes, limited in its scope to the protection of children. Whether it should be applied to all other classes of illegal immigrants is a matter that the courts have yet to decide. I think it unlikely that the courts would rule that Congress is barred from prohibiting illegal residents from working or obtaining welfare benefits.

The more substantive argument is a moral one. Fiss argues that distinctions between citizens and non-citizens turn both legal and illegal immigrants into "social pariahs," and that to deny benefits to any class of non-citizens is to impose social disabilities upon that group. Fiss recognizes that by calling for an end to such distinctions he may appear to be questioning the validity of laws regulating immigration. He denies, however, that his intention is to subvert the admission process. "Admission laws," he writes, "can be enforced by fences at the borders, deportation proceedings, or criminal sanctions, not, I maintain, by imposing social disabilities." He says he does not question the validity of laws regulating admissions, and he is prepared to assume "for present purposes" that they are just.

One must address the question, then, of whether the abolition of the distinction between citizens and all classes of non-citizens residing in the United States does not, in effect, create an open-border policy. What if all of the twenty-five million individuals who enter the United States each year could seek employment and obtain the same welfare and educational benefits as citizens? Employment opportunities are the single most important determinant of illegal migration to the United States. As long as jobs are available and wages in the United States are higher than in other countries individuals from abroad will try to gain entry into the U.S. labor market.

Fiss is no doubt right in noting that individuals who are illegally employed are socially disabled. Reports abound of Mexican, Chinese, and Thai illegal immigrants in sweatshops and in servitude, forced to pay back traffickers in unlawful entry and lacking the legal means to protect themselves against unscrupulous employers. Workers cannot complain about wages or working conditions if their employers can threaten them with deportation. Legalizing illegal immigrants' right to work seems like an obvious solution, except that one cannot make employment legal for those whose residence is illegal. If anyone in the United States, including short-term visitors, is free to work, we will have created the single most important incentive for illegal migration and at the same time we will have ended the only viable instrument for detecting and deporting illegal immigrants other than interdiction at sea and at our borders. Indeed, border controls would be of little or no value. As it is, half the illegal immigrants in the United States already *enter* legally; they simply remain here after their visas have expired. The alternative to legalizing employment for illegal immigrants is to enforce existing legislation imposing penalties on employers for hiring them, but Congress has thus far been unwilling to put in place a national system for identifying citizens and others who are legally entitled to work.

Should illegal immigrants have access to the welfare system and to other social benefits? There is no evidence that public benefits draw in illegal immigrants. Denying emergency medical care to illegals creates risks to public health. Denying education to the children of illegal immigrants impairs the development of people who may become long-term residents. And denying access to emergency medical care and education undermines the trust necessary for the functioning of essential services. But these considerations do not pertain to all social benefits. When public policy aims to induce illegal immigrants to return home or be deported, it makes no sense to provide them with Medicaid or Supplementary Security Income.

The broader question is whether illegal immigrants should enjoy the same social benefits as citizens and legally admitted immigrants. To answer it, we might begin with the principle that social benefits are acquired through membership in a community. The sharing of social benefits and the transfer of income payments from one individual to another is within a community and is not automatically extended to those who do not belong to that community. But now we need to ask who belongs to the community. Simply being here does not make one a member. The list of criteria for community membership includes citizenship, by birth or by naturalization. We welcome immigrants into our community as citizens once they meet a variety of conditions, and we also welcome refugees and asylees (people who have been admitted temporarily because of conditions in their country of origin). Though not (yet) members of the community, refugees and asylees are nonetheless entitled to the full panoply of social benefits (plus some assistance not provided to others) because they are in need of protection and are, for the time being, unable to return home safely. If illegal immigrants are not caught and deported, then in time (how much time?) they and their children acquire de facto membership in the community. A humane policy is one which regularizes their status.

Should legal immigrants then have access to all the benefits of citizenship short of voting rights? Most rights and benefits are extended to immigrants in order to enable them to become full members of the community—with equal rights to employment, education, housing, and welfare benefits. But there is a long-standing view in the United States that immigrants should not become a public charge except under very limited circumstances. The Commission on Immigration Reform, chaired by the late Barbara Jordan, argued that sponsors who provide the financial guarantees to allow an immigrant to enter should be held financially accountable for that person. Naturalized citizens and immigrants who sponsor their elderly parents, for example, should be responsible for their parents' financial support at least until the latter become citizens. Similarly, the sponsors of spouses and children should assume financial responsibility for those persons for the duration of the familial relationship or for a specified period.

The current rules with respect to benefits—and we have barely scratched the surface with regard to their complexity—are often unclear and inconsistent. One reason for this is that these rules serve a variety of diverse objectives. We want policies that will deter illegal immigrants, reduce the costs of the welfare system, prevent immigrants from becoming public charges, enable immigrants to become full members of the community, assist refugees and asylees (including those awaiting determination of their status), and treat children and others in need of protection humanely. Given these varied public objectives and the trade-offs among them, we need a deliberative legislative process, or an immigration service or commission, that can formulate clearer and more consistent rules than those we now have. Alas, our fragmented policymaking system, as it relates to immigration issues, makes the creation of coherent policies difficult. Still, our present policies are not all that bad, and in our usual messy fashion we are trying to sort out who should get what. What we don't need—at the expense of workers and taxpayers—is the kind of solution offered by Fiss: that everyone present within the boundaries of the United States ought to have the same rights and benefits. It would be politically irresponsible to turn these legislative issues over to the courts to decide on the basis of constitutional principles. Instead, we need reasoned analysis and public discussion of how we can balance diverse objectives to accomplish what is fiscally possible, what is humane, and what best serves the goals of incorporating immigrants into citizenship, deterring illegals, maintaining public health, and protecting children.

Getting Policy
Exactly Wrong

JAGDISH BHAGWATI

*O*wen Fiss makes my day. For some years now, in a series of essays, book reviews, and op-ed articles,[1] I have
argued for an immigration policy that would shift enforcement to the border while effectively reducing, or at
least freezing, the current level of internal enforcement
aimed at punishing employers of illegal immigrants (via
employer sanctions) and the illegals themselves (via I.D.
cards, INS raids with a view to detection, detention, and
deportation, et al.). A bipartisan consensus, however, has
moved increasingly in the opposite direction by zeroing
in on the illegals already in our midst, not just through
punishments but even (for many) by denying them access to social benefits assured to all Americans. Despite
this trajectory, I remained optimistic that I would not be
lonely for too long. Frankly, I had expected my fellow
economists and political scientists to move in my direction. Instead, Owen Fiss brings constitutional law to
bear on the issue, lending me a wholly unforeseen and
entirely welcome ally.

Two Policy Objectives

Broadly speaking, enlightened Americans share two principal objectives in their conception of an appropriate policy towards illegal immigration: to reduce the illegal inflow and to treat people who are here—whether native or naturalized or alien—with the basic decency that each of us owes to others within the community. This fundamental good sense defines our obligations as much as their rights.

The first objective is typical of nearly all societies: borders are commonly defined to exclude, and borders out of control simply do not sit well with the body politic. But the second objective is, at least in intensity, uniquely American. Other modern societies also exhibit elements of such a concern, but rarely with our passion and consistency.

The explanation lies in our history: the absence of an identity defined by shared memories that define "us" against "others," and a history of immigration that leads the culture to pride itself on ensuring chances for each and all. Our collective sensibility is offended at its core when we contemplate that any group, any individual, is denied fair access to the opportunities that our country offers.[2] Thus the notion that we can live alongside an underclass of humanity, whose members are denied access to social benefits and economic betterment simply because they are illegal aliens, violates our fundamental sense of decency and morality.[3]

A False Start

Our legislators have typically tried to achieve these twin objectives by eliminating illegals who are already here: the first objective having been fully achieved, the second would follow as well, since you could not ill-treat illegals if there were none. To that end, efforts have been made since the 1986 immigration reform legislation to reduce the number of illegals through an amnesty program, and to reduce the flow of new illegals through employer sanctions that would eliminate the magnet of employment opportunity.

Predictably, however, the amnesty program left many people still in illegal status. More important, employer sanctions could not reduce the flow of new illegal immigrants. Even in Germany and Switzerland, government analyses had warned, such sanctions face serious enforcement problems since few judges would impose the necessary penalties against employers whose only sin was hiring (as against ill-treating and exploiting) illegal workers. In the United States, our strong civil liberties traditions and organizations raised the enforcement hurdle even higher. Besides, for many individuals, the difference between their prospects in their home countries and those in the United States are so vast that employer sanctions could not seriously reduce incentives to attempt illegal entry.

In effect, then, the illegals continued in our midst, with little change in the number of attempted entries: the first objective was hardly advanced. At the same time, INS harassment increased with enhanced domestic enforcement, pushing even more illegal immigrants into the underclass, so even the second objective was set back. The 1986 consensus on policy had plainly been wrong.[4]

CURRENT FOLLIES

The answer, therefore, must be to turn the policy on its head. Try to control immigration at the border. To be sure, this strategy will not work too well because more than half the illegals (according to our best estimates) now come across in difficult-to-monitor ways other than crossing the Rio Grande. But such enforcement will produce the satisfaction, at low cost, that "we are trying to control the influx." As to the illegals who are here, treat them like us: leave them alone more rather than less. And permit them to enjoy our social and economic rights.

But instead, we have again worked ourselves up into a frenzy, seeking ever more domestic enforcement in addition to employer sanctions. There have been increasing demands to deny illegal immigrants (even legal immigrants, at times) access to social benefits in the tired and false expectation that these policies will significantly reduce the incentive for attempted entries. So we see the prospect of more domestic enforcement that will do little to reduce illegal inflows and much to drive illegals into an underclass that degrades them and offends our moral sensibilities, while also, according to Fiss's analysis, violating the Constitution.

PETE WILSON MEETS "HARVARD SQUARE"

Two recent developments have hastened this movement to the brink. First, whether Pete Wilson was also motivated by his own animus against illegals and/or a low-politics pandering to his constituents' animus, there is no question that California had fiscal problems, problems analogous to those in Texas and Florida. While illegal immigrants create a net (if mild) fiscal surplus, immigration studies reveal a distributional problem: the federal government gains net revenue and the states lose it. This fiscal problem for states results in part from the educational expenditures which were in contention in *Plyler v. Doe* (see Fiss's article for analysis of this case). Efforts by state legislatures to exclude illegals from social benefits might, then, be viewed as a political strategy aimed at generating federal assistance for these states. Because immigration policy is a federal matter, I should think the federal government does have constitutional responsibilities in this area. But let me leave it at that.

Far more worrisome is the unfortunate intellectual role played by economists and sociologists. Two of their arguments have helped turn the illegal immigration "phenomenon" into a "problem": (a) because illegals are typically undereducated and unskilled, their presence has been a contributory factor in the decline in real wages of our own unskilled workers since the 1980s; and (b) inner-city problems have been exacerbated by the fact that these immigrants take jobs that would otherwise have gone to natives. As it happens, many of these social scientists are currently located in Cambridge, Massachusetts, and can be aptly described as the "Harvard Square" school of nay-sayers. Among the economists is George Borjas of Harvard's John F. Kennedy School of Government, who drew media attention as Pete Wilson's adviser.[5] Among the sociologists are Orlando Patterson and Kathleen Newman, now at the Kennedy School. Patterson has drawn on Borjas's economics to urge President Clinton to take on illegals more strenuously. Newman's remarkable work on the problems of the inner city has correctly emphasized the importance of economic opportunity for blacks, but is unfortunately often interpreted as implying a substitutional relationship between blacks and unskilled immigrants.

I have no space to say why these arguments are unconvincing: Francisco Rivera-Batiz and I are just finishing a book entitled *In the Eye of the Storm: Targeting Illegal Aliens*, where we refute these alarming contentions both conceptually and empirically.

But I may add that many of these intellectuals have been led to the non sequitur that we must encourage skilled immigrants at the expense of unskilled ones. This proposal is not merely economically indefensible (since it is impossible to make a convincing case that skilled immigrants will produce greater benefits for us) but also violates our deepest moral sense. Suppose we had only one place for an immigrant, and could give it to a rich doctor from India or an impoverished peasant from Haiti. Suppose you are to vote entirely on the basis of whom you wish to assist and not on which immigrant will do *you* good. Which would you choose? I have little doubt that the average American would choose the impoverished peasant. The Statue of Liberty does capture that essential truth about us; and it is that truth which is obscured by a focus in the scholarly debate upon what is materially good for us and by the unconvincing economics often deployed to support alarmist views.

Rights or Privileges?

MUZAFFAR CHISHTI

$\mathcal{T}$o those who are concerned about principles of constitutional law and political morality, Owen Fiss has issued a timely reminder. Excluding the narrow world of immigration lawyers—and the remarkably persistent attention given the issue by *New York Times* columnist Anthony Lewis—the damage done by Congress[1] in the name of immigration reform has not received the serious public scrutiny that it deserves.

But, curiously, the most serious damage—not just to immigrants but to the principles of constitutional law— is not mentioned in Fiss's essay. I am referring here to the wholesale denial of due process of law in most immigration proceedings, the elimination of judicial review of immigration agency actions, and the retroactive application of laws. These developments are deeply troubling and raise more fundamental constitutional issues than those highlighted by Fiss.

Fiss's list of social disabilities is also less alarming than he suggests, for one simple reason: most of these disabilities have been remedied. Congress, after all, voted against "federalizing" California's Proposition 187, reversed the bar on Supplementary Security Income and Medicaid to the elderly, and partially restored food stamps to legal immigrants. These are not small gains, especially during a period seen as the political heyday of the current anti-immigrant movement.

These caveats aside, however, Fiss's analysis does justice to some major issues in today's immigration debate.

I am instinctively sympathetic to the argument that social disability can invite constitutional scrutiny. I am in complete agreement that Fiss's list of social disabilities raises fundamental constitutional issues when it is applied to lawful permanent residents. I do not, however, believe that the same is true when it is applied to illegal immigrants.

I come to this view because I believe that there is a fundamental difference between rights and benefits. Fiss's list constitutes benefits, not rights. Benefits merit a different analysis—especially when they have financial costs associated with them. The same principle that Fiss applies to the political privilege of voting, I believe, applies to the privilege of receiving benefits: the principle of rules of membership. For states that have to make choices among competing claimants for finite resources, it is appropriate to ask for some evidence of attachment—or membership—in the society before providing benefits to an immigrant. Lawful presence in the country is an acceptable minimum criterion for such membership.

There are, however, two public benefits for which even illegal immigrants must be eligible: basic public education and emergency medical care. These can be defended more on grounds of societal interest than benefit to the immigrant; untreated diseases and unattended vulnerable children present concrete costs and dangers to the larger society.

On the other hand, the rights of illegal aliens deserve a different treatment. One's position on illegal immigration can and should be distinct from the position one takes on the rights of illegal immigrants. Some rights have to be respected without regard to immigration status. The right to due process of law and to judicial review fall in this category. Similarly, to borrow Fiss's principle of antisubjugation, illegal immigrants must be protected from acts that promote subjugation. This is especially true in the workplace, where lack of rights can result in private economic gains to unscrupulous employers. Workplace laws must apply to all workers, without regard to status. Without that protection, employers have additional incentives to hire and exploit illegal aliens.

I would like to conclude with a comment on Fiss's comparison of the political powerlessness of immigrants and that of insular minorities like blacks. Immigration status, as Fiss points out, is not permanent in the same sense that race is. Nor is the powerlessness of immigrants. Ironically, one reason that many of the most severe social disabilities created by the congressional legislation of 1996 have been reversed is the extraordinary political power that newly naturalized citizens have demonstrated since that time. If Proposition 187 was the high point of the current anti-immigrant movement, it also managed to turn the politics of immigration on its head. Anti-immigrant rhetoric has suddenly stopped yielding political rewards. Fresh citizens are voting in large numbers and they are exacting a price for anti-immigrant policies. And politicians of all stripes are paying attention.

※ III ※

Reply: A Third Reconstruction?

OWEN FISS

*T*hese are dark and difficult days. The economy is flourishing, but the spirit is mean. Rather than using the freedom that prosperity brings to extend an extra hand to the needy, we seem determined, as Rogers Smith put it, "to shore up rotting but still deeply entrenched timbers of our old politically crafted racial and ethnic hierarchies." Smith's observation applies with particular force to the treatment of immigrants.

In "The Immigrant as Pariah," I sought to counter this trend and to explain why recent measures affecting immigrants are inconsistent with the constitutional principle condemning caste. I turned to the judiciary for the implementation of that principle, and in so doing, reflected a certain unease—detected by a number of the respondents—about organized politics as the avenue for the pursuit of justice. My critics are right when they say that politics need not be reduced to the pursuit of self-interest and can be a domain for the discharge of our moral responsibilities, but the sad truth is that far too often other, less attractive considerations come into play and the results are utterly deplorable.

A case in point is the June 1998 amendment—extolled by Myron Weiner, Muzaffar Chishti, and others—to the federal welfare act of 1996. While this amendment enables needy immigrants who are disabled to obtain food stamps, thereby moderating the harshness of the welfare law, it only is applicable if these individuals can show that they lawfully entered the United States before August 22, 1996 (the date of the enactment of the 1996 law), and, even more bizarrely, that their disability arose prior to that date. Jennifer Gordon proposes that immigrants be given some participatory rights, but such reforms are unlikely to preclude results such as those embodied in the 1998 or 1996 statutes or to transform politics into, borrowing Ronald Dworkin's phrase, a forum of principle.

But if we cannot expect much from politics, why have high hopes for judicial decisions? Judges are, as John Ely once reminded us, people, and suffer all the human foibles. The exercise of judicial power is limited, however, by certain procedural norms that have no counterpart in politics. I refer here not just to the independence of the judiciary from the will of the electorate, so uncharitable these days, but also to the requirements that judges must respond to grievances that they might otherwise prefer to ignore, hear from all aggrieved parties, assume individual responsibility for their decisions, and justify their decisions in terms of publicly accepted norms. Judges engage in a special dialogue with the public. Through this dialogue they achieve a certain distance from their personal proclivities and come face to face with what Mark Tushnet might call universal reason.

Sometimes this faith in reason proves justified, as it did one bright and sunny day in 1954. The exercise of judicial reason in *Brown v. Board of Education* did not, reading Robin West's fears back into history, divest the political agencies of their responsibility. Rather, it acted as a catalyst, a call to action, to which all the nation, including the President and Congress, responded, first to enforce that decision and then to extend it. The 1960s were marked by a coordination, rather than a separation, of powers, and the Court was very much at the helm, though no one should slight the contribution of various political agencies or ordinary citizens, who often took to the streets or voiced their grievances in the halls of justice or before the bar of politics.

The antisubjugation principle emerged from this extraordinary process of reform, which came to be known as the Second Reconstruction. Ulrich Preuss underscores the exceptional nature of what the Court was then attempting and the task I envision for the judiciary in my article. From the German perspective, it is unimaginable that the courts would, in his words, "correct society's structural deficiencies." This is precisely, however, what *Brown* attempted and is a source of the uniqueness and greatness of the American constitutional tradition.

Alexander Aleinikoff warmly endorses this tradition and the undertaking begun in *Brown*, but urges that the principle of that case, specifically the rule against subjugation, be confined to remedying the plight of African-Americans. Immigrants should be content with anti-discrimination. In drawing this distinction, he slights the multitude of connections—underscored by many participants in this symposium, most notably Rogers Smith, Richard Freeman, and Iris Young—between racial hierarchies and the social structures that subjugate other groups, including immigrants or those defined in terms of income, gender, language, sexual orientation, or disability. He overlooks the essential unity of equality. The Second Reconstruction began with race, as indeed was right and proper, since our treatment of blacks represented the greatest betrayal of the principles of the Constitution, but was soon extended to other disadvantaged groups.

Some of my critics embrace the antisubjugation principle and acknowledge its applicability to legal immigrants, but deny that it affords any protection to illegal immigrants. Such a view treats illegal immigrants as though they were transitory visitors, or, to borrow Iris Young's phrase, "alien invaders," overlooking the multitude of connections that bind the newcomers to the community in which they chose to make their lives. Young acknowledges one set of connections—specifically the social and economic ones—but ignores those that form the basis for the jurisdiction of the Constitution. She denies the significance of the nation-state—

for her, there is little difference between residents of San Diego and Tijuana. Yet this is precisely the domain governed by the Constitution. The Constitution speaks to the nation, not to the world, and establishes the principles by which the nation is to be governed. While Young's visionary regionalism is indeed moving, fully justifying the construction of institutions that might dispense transnational justice, it should never be understood in a way that would undercut the claim vindicated by the Supreme Court's decision in *Plyler v. Doe*, which indeed recognized that all those who make their lives in the United States, even those who may have once entered illegally, are members of the constitutional community.

Plyler gave constitutional life to the self-understanding of America that is symbolized by the Statue of Liberty and our reverence for it. It expresses, in Jagdish Bhagwati's words, an "essential truth" about ourselves as a nation. That decision was handed down in 1982, and admittedly it was more of a sign of the past than an indication of where the Court was heading. By the mid-1970s, the Court had already abandoned the project begun in *Brown*. Congress filled the void during the 1970s and 1980s, and in fact countered many of the judicial setbacks to civil rights during that period, but it dramatically reversed course after the 1994 elections. It is now pursuing a different path altogether. The White House withdrew from the civil rights coalition after the election of President Nixon in 1968, and with the exception of the

Carter intermezzo, remained hostile to egalitarianism throughout the 1970s and 1980s. The election of President Clinton in 1992 was cause for some hope, but by August 1996, when he signed the welfare bill that is at the center of this symposium, it became clear, all *too* clear, that the reform effort known as the Second Reconstruction was at an end.

Much of the work of the Second Reconstruction remains unfinished. This endeavor achieved notable successes for African-Americans in enlarging the franchise, opening the doors of public accommodations, and integrating the upper echelons of society. It also improved the positions of women and the handicapped. For other disadvantaged groups—like immigrants, the immediate focus of my article—the subordinating structures have been reinforced. All the respondents are unified in the thought that the present Court is unlikely to accept the full force of the *Plyler* decision and give substance to its underlying principle, much less issue a call for a third reconstruction. I do not disagree.

I am impelled, however, by a commitment to reason and a certain vision of the responsibilities of intellectuals in these troubled times. Our task is not to anticipate the response of the Court, even less that of the political branches, but to address the great issues of the day and to discover and then explain what justice requires, with the hope that some day and in some way the truth will find a home in this world. We have to begin somewhere.

Notes

Edwidge Danticat / *Foreword*

1. See Owen Fiss, "The Immigrant as Pariah," 11.
2. See Jagdish Bhagwati, "Getting Policy Wrong."

Rogers M. Smith / *Caste Recast*

1. Peter Brimelow, *Alien Nation: Common Sense About America's Immigration Disaster* (New York: Random House, 1995), 1, 58–59, 122, 217–19, 263–64.
2. Richard J. Herrnstein and Charles Murray, *The Bell Curve: Intelligence and Class Structure in American Life* (New York: The Free Press, 1994), 356–64, 479–526.

Jennifer Gordon / *Let Them Vote*

1. Readers interested in in-depth historical and legal analyses of some of the points touched on in this article should see articles on non-citizen voting by Sanford Levinson, Gerald Neuman, Jamin Raskin, and Gerald Rosberg; this piece owes a debt to all of their work.

Mark Tushnet / *Open Borders*

1. Annette Baier, "Some Virtues of Resident Alienage," in *Virtue*, NOMOS XIV, ed. John W. Chapman and William A. Galston (New York: NYU Press, 1992), 291.

2. Martha Nussbaum, "Patriotism and Cosmopolitanism," *Boston Review* 19, no. 5 (October/November 1994); reprinted in Martha Nussbaum, *For Love of Country* (Boston: Beacon Press, 1996).

JAGDISH BHAGWATI / *Getting Policy Exactly Wrong*

1. Several of these have been reprinted in my latest book, *A Stream of Windows: Reflections on Trade, Immigration and Democracy* (Cambridge, Massachusetts: MIT Press, 1998); see especially chapters 31–34 and 39.

2. Yes, there are serious lapses, especially in regard to blacks. But here too the strength of the civil rights movement, and our ability to make steady if inadequate progress towards equality of access for the black community, are reflections of what I argue in the text. So is the fact that when seized by panic over the rise of Japan in world trade, the Europeans simply erected significant barriers against Japan without any angst whatsoever, whereas we had to go through a song and dance about how "unfair" the Japanese were in trade, thus first convincing ourselves that striking the Japanese with trade sanctions and barriers was a "fair" move on our part! On the Japan question, and how we handled it as described, see again *A Stream of Windows*, especially chapters 14–16 and 18–21.

3. This sentiment surfaces in a much weaker sense in other civilized societies, simply because it is difficult to come down hard on hapless humanity. I have often cited a telling quote from the Swiss novelist Max Frisch, who, on observing how West Europeans found it extremely difficult to send home the *gastarbeiteren* (guestworkers) even though they had been brought in on the explicit understanding that they could be sent back, remarked, "We imported workers and got men instead."

4. This is just what I had anticipated; see my *Wall Street Journal* article of 1 February 1985, reprinted as Chapter 33 in *A Stream of Windows*.

5. Borjas has been arguing that the immigration of unskilled workers has harmed our workers' wages; Dani Rodrik of the Kennedy School has endorsed the related claim that trade with poor

countries has harmed our workers (see his 1997 pamphlet *Has Global-ization Gone Too Far?*). I have challenged both assertions in my own recent research.

Muzaffar Chishti / *Rights or Privileges?*

1. Here I mean the combined effect of three pieces of legislation that Congress passed in 1996: the Welfare Reform Act, the Illegal Immigration Reform and Individual Responsibility Act, and the Anti-terrorism and Effective Death Penalty Act.

ABOUT THE CONTRIBUTORS

T. ALEXANDER ALEINIKOFF teaches at the Georgetown University Law Center and is a senior associate at the International Migration Policy Program of the Carnegie Endowment for International Peace. From 1994 to 1997 he was general counsel and executive associate commissioner of the Immigration and Naturalization Service.

JAGDISH BHAGWATI is the Arthur Lehman Professor of Economics and a professor of political science at Columbia University. His most recent book is *A Stream of Windows: Unsettling Reflections on Trade, Immigration and Democracy.*

MUZAFFAR CHISHTI is a lawyer and the director of the immigration project at the Union of Needletrades, Industrial and Textile Employees (UNITE).

OWEN FISS is Sterling Professor of Law at Yale University. His most recent books are *Liberalism Divided* and *The Irony of Free Speech.*

RICHARD B. FREEMAN holds the Ascherman Chair of Economics at Harvard University. He is program director in labor studies at the National Bureau of Economic Research and executive director of the Programme for Discontinuous Economics at the London School of Economics Center for Economic Performance.

JENNIFER GORDON is the founder and former executive director of the Workplace Project, a center that organizes immigrant workers in New York. She is currently an Open Society Institute individual project fellow writing about immigrants, law, and organizing.

ULRICH K. PREUSS is a professor of law and politics at the Free University Berlin and a judge at the constitutional court of the state of Bremen.

ROGERS M. SMITH is a professor of political science at Yale University. His *Civic Ideals: Conflicting Visions of Citizenship in U.S. History* was a finalist for the 1998 Pulitzer Prize in history.

About the Contributors

MARK TUSHNET teaches constitutional law at the Georgetown University Law Center. His forthcoming book is *Taking the Constitution Away from the Courts.*

MYRON WEINER is a professor of political science and former director of the Center for International Studies at the Massachusetts Institute of Technology. His books include *The Global Migration Crisis.*

ROBIN WEST is a professor of law at the Georgetown University Law Center and the author of *Caring for Justice.*

IRIS YOUNG is a professor of public and international affairs at the University of Pittsburgh. Her most recent book is *Intersecting Voices: Dilemmas of Gender, Political Philosophy, and Policy.*